LETTERS ON PREACHING

WILLIAM WAND

Letters on Preaching

HODDER AND STOUGHTON
LONDON SYDNEY AUCKLAND TORONTO

Contents

Maries prerogative was to beare Christ, so
'Tis preachers to convey him, for they doe
As Angels out of clouds, from Pulpits speake,
And bless the poore beneathe, the lame, the weake.

John Donne

Though I speak with the tongues of men and of angels,
and have not charity, I am become as sounding brass,
or a tinkling cymbal.

St. Paul

An Invitation Accepted

My dear Robert,

You put me on the spot when you ask me to write you some full-length letters on preaching. You see, preaching is so personal a thing: it implies putting oneself at the public disposal in respect of the truth one holds dearest in life. Curiously enough, in the course of time it becomes easy, perhaps too easy, to do this, so to speak, professionally, from the pulpit. But I think it must always be difficult to perform such an act of self-vivisection in the private company of one single individual, especially when that individual is a relative.

However, your request is one that I could not refuse. All true students are ready to help each other—it is one of the marks of the trade—and in this subject one remains a student to the end of one's life. It would ill become one who is at the end of his career to withhold the benefit of his experience from a young man who has not yet entered upon his. At the same time you flatter me when you base your request on the length of my experience.

To admit that one has been preaching for seventy years is not likely to be much of a commendation in days when novelty is at a premium, and when even vendors of patent medicines and soap powders find their sales fall off if they cannot proclaim that their products are something 'new'. But the truth must out: I did begin preaching as a schoolboy of eighteen, helping out a local vicar who was short of a curate to serve on Sunday evenings in his mission. And I still continue at the age of eighty-nine to preach when neighbouring clergy are kind enough to invite me.

In any case he would be a poor sort of preacher who did not adapt his method to the changing times. If his essential message is eternal, his way of presenting it must meet the needs of each passing generation. Inasmuch as the average congregation spans several generations, there is something to be said for listening on occasion to one who in his own experience spans more generations than most.

Well, I seem to be launching into my subject already. I hope you will forgive me if sometimes I seem to treat you as if you were the class of ordinands to whom I used to lecture half a century ago, while at other times I drop into that style of personal reminiscence from which the elderly seldom escape. In our particular circumstances the alternation between the donnish and the avuncular is, I am afraid, almost inevitable. In any case I don't think a few anecdotes are likely to do you much harm; and they still have the power to amuse me.

You will realise that this short letter is only by way of introduction. You will have to put up with something much more bulky later on.

The Foolishness of Preaching

My dear Robert,

I did once meditate the writing of a book on preaching, and even got so far as hesitating between two possible titles. The one was *The Foolishness of Preaching*, and the other *Preaching as an Art*. Both of them seemed to me to say something significant, the former naturally so, because it is from no less an author than St. Paul himself (1 Cor. 1:21). It is not his own phrase but one to which he takes the strongest exception. It represents the Greeks' attack, not on the manner but on the substance of preaching. The Apostle asserts that what the Greeks thought foolishness was in point of fact the wisdom and the power of God. It was God's good pleasure through the 'foolishness' of the thing preached to save those who believed. Paul, like the British soldiers long after him (cf. 'contemptibles', 'desert rats'), took the opprobrious terms hurled at him by his opponents and used them as honorific titles. He quite simply *boasted* of the preaching that took an executed criminal as its subject.

About this foolishness of preaching I hope to say something in the present letter. About preaching as an art I shall write at length in my next instalment. But there are some preliminaries to face first.

The first thing to do is to make sure that we know what we are talking about. According to Bultmann and the existentialists, 'preaching' means 'challenge'. That is an opinion which, coming from such a source, merits careful consideration.

Actually the Greek word which in the New Testament is translated by 'preaching' is *kerygma*, and it meant originally 'proclamation'. In classical times it was used of an announcement by a herald. So under Christian influence the apostle or other person appointed to preach was regarded as a herald sent by the King of Kings to proclaim the good news or gospel. In our context, preaching is still essentially the proclamation of the good news of salvation.

As Horton Davies, speaking of the preacher as a herald of God, says in his *Varieties of English Preaching*, page 209,

> He is supremely the ambassador of the King of Kings, announcing through the authority of his calling and ordination by God the good news of Christ's victory over the world and offering the grace of pardon to repentant sinners.

No doubt the proclamation implies a challenge. Every hearer of a sermon is expected to do something about what he hears. The news is of so earth-shaking a quality that one cannot just sit and listen to it as if one were in the audience at some sort of dramatic recital. We can either accept it as true or reject it as false, but we cannot remain indifferent to it. If it is true, we must be up and doing: if it is false, we must at least give our moral support to the fraud squad.

This implication of the *kerygma* is difficult to realise as one sits somnolent in the accustomed pew Sunday by Sunday, lulled by the gentle voice of an elderly preacher reading carefully from a close-written manuscript. We have heard it all so often; we have been brought up to it; we know it well; we are immunised against any sting its familiar phrases may still conceal. But one day, perhaps for no obvious reason, something clicks; the alarm goes off; we are stabbed broad awake; we really hear the good news as news; the proclamation sounds in our inner ear, and is translated forthwith into an epoch-making challenge.

But here is the rub. Just because the challenge is epoch-making it cannot maintain its existence as challenge. Once we have passed into the new epoch the precise quality of challenge is over: henceforth the preaching must take on a new quality. If we have the curiosity to look into the dictionaries, we shall find this change corroborated in the somewhat different definition that is given to the English term 'preaching'. Dr. Johnson, for instance, says, "Preaching: to pronounce a public discourse on sacred subjects". And no one seems to have improved much upon that.

To go back for a moment to the Greek: what was the function of the *kerux* or herald? He was the man whose duty it was to announce public proclamations—a sort of town-crier in fact. In the secular sphere no qualification was originally demanded of him but that he should have a good voice. This endowment became less necessary as his duties were extended to include ambassadorial functions. The change was facilitated by the fact that in the sphere of religion the mystery cults already had their own heralds to assist in their worship. At the same time ambassadors were regarded as being under the special protection of God, so that from both spheres, secular and religious, the herald achieved a certain status of sanctity.

In Jewry there was no official whose duties corresponded to those of the Greek *kerux*. That, no doubt, is why the Septuagint uses the term no more than four times, twice in the Old Testament and twice in the Apocrypha. Even the New Testament contains only three instances of its use, twice of St. Paul and once of Noah.

It has been suggested that the Bible uses the term so little just because, while the pagan herald was so sacrosanct an official, the Jewish or Christian preacher was a humble person, who might easily be persecuted and even done to death. In the latter case it is the message that lives on; and so the New Testament redresses the balance by stressing the action rather than the office, the verb rather than the noun: if we hear little of the herald or *kerux*, we hear a good deal of heralding or preaching (*kerussein*). There are also a host of other synonyms such as 'confess', 'proclaim', 'declare', 'publish', and, the favourite of all, 'announce good news', which takes us into the very heart of the Christian proclamation of the gospel.

No doubt all these terms showed a tendency to lose their sharp edge in common speech. Even in current English we can reply to the too-anxious admonitions of a relative or friend, "Don't preach at me", or we can say of a moralising author, "He preaches too much." But we still know what is meant by the sermon of a duly constituted preacher: it is at least an exhortation with a moral content. Even so, it has declined from what it was at the outset: the proclamation of good news, the good news of salvation through Christ.

As I have already suggested, some change was, in the course of time, inevitable. Almost from the beginning, moral exhortation was added as a corollary to the news. But this did not relieve preachers from keeping the news as fresh as possible. News does not remain news for long. Even a nine days' wonder cannot be proclaimed as news when that period has expired. Indeed, the cynics go much further and say of something in which the public has ceased to take any interest that it is 'as dead as yesterday's news'; and the evening papers will regard what the morning papers have said as 'dead as mutton'. If the birth, death and resurrection of Jesus Christ are still news in the twentieth century, it can only be to the freshly awakened soul who has been brought to realise for the first time the full implication of what, to him as an individual, the familiar story of Christ may truly mean.

Happy the preacher who can still make the old story come vividly alive to his hearers! I realised this with particular poignancy in France during the First World War. I was standing on the edge of the crowd listening to Studdert Kennedy preaching in a vast railway shed to the troops on their way to the front. As we turned away at the conclusion of the address, I heard a tall Guardee sergeant say to his companion, "My word, that chap's got a heart, hasn't he?" It reminded me of something said to me by another soldier, who in peace time was a schoolmaster: "You know, until I heard Kennedy preach I never realised that the sermon meant anything. Listening to the old Vicar at home, I thought it was just part of the ritual."

No doubt in the case of that particular preacher the effect was produced at least partly through the apparent ease and spontaneity with which he spoke. That his speaking was not truly spontaneous I knew very well, for once when he was preparing his Sunday evening sermon he had asked me to run through his typescript for him. But his essential sincerity and his real love of people were strong enough to break through the restraint that might have been imposed upon him by too meticulous preparation.

In his case, too, the proclamation of the gospel was nicely mingled with moral exhortation, and that of a type that showed a thorough understanding of the human situation. This combination of proclamation and moral exhortation has become common form with modern preachers. It has been demanded of them by the laity, who are wont to insist upon what they call 'practical' sermons, by which they mean discourses that do not leave doctrines hanging in the air but reveal their relevance to everyday life. And that can hardly be done without dwelling upon moral issues.

Such touching upon life at many points led logically to the inclusion of a third element in the sermon, that of teaching. People must *know* before they can *do*. In any case they need some intellectual support for their faith. And always there is also a natural curiosity to be satisfied. Thus, explanations of the Bible together with studies of doctrine and church history began to form a natural element, along with morals and proclamation, as possible sources for preaching material.

It is true that modern scholarship distinguishes very sharply between preaching and teaching (*kerygma* and *didache*) as they are found in the New Testament. That is a useful distinction in the context of biblical studies, helping us to contrast the historical with the theological elements of the text and so providing us with a fresh understanding of our foundation documents. But in the context in which we are now working, that of the pulpit, such a contrast had best be forgotten, or at least it should not be allowed to develop into open conflict between the two. A 'teaching' sermon may or may not be as popular as a 'practical' one, but there are few preachers who would not agree that it is equally necessary.

This is perhaps enough for an opening letter. It will in any case give you something to think about in connection with this most important element of a minister's task. John Donne in his *Letter to Mr. Tilman after he had taken Orders* describes the preachers speaking from their pulpits as 'angels out of clouds'. This is not intended to be taken humorously. Donne had a high conception of the preachers' office and thought that their message from the pulpit should come with something of the same authority as the voices from heaven at Jesus's birth and at various points in his ministry.

Preaching as an Art

My dear Robert,

In my last letter I half suggested that our subject might be
limited within the phrase 'preaching as an Art'. Continuing the
effort to define our terms, we should now go on to ask what in
this connection we mean by 'art'. Certainly the term is not
usually regarded as wide enough to include preaching. Looking
through my copy of *The Times* this morning, I see that page 17
is devoted to art, but when I turn to that page I look in vain for
a sermon. There is a section on opera, a piece about the piano,
an article on bridge, and even something about bayonets for
boys, but no sign here of any interest in preaching. True, there
is a sermon, and a good one too, but it is on a quite different
page, hard by the court circular. That no doubt takes us back to
its regal beginnings when the preacher was a royal herald, but
it shows no relation between preaching and art. Nevertheless, I
adhere firmly to the belief that the sermon is a form of art.

The nature of art is best understood through its contrast with
science. Science is what you know: art is what you do. The
basic idea of art appears to be that of skill. What is done well,
with taste, discernment and craftsmanship is art. Another
dimension of the meaning can be seen in its contrast with
nature. Art is distinguished from nature by the fact that it is the
product of human energy and ingenuity. Nature is what comes
directly, or through some evolutionary process, from the
Creator. Art can only be derived from the hand of man. True
art is distinguished from artificiality by not making its human

origin too obvious. *Ars est celare artem.* If the hand of the maker is too clearly seen, the product leads us to think of the producer, and the artefact is no longer able to claim judgment for what it is in itself. That is why art demands taste as well as discernment and craftsmanship. It is universally agreed that it shows bad taste, vulgarity, for the maker to obtrude himself.

The unreflecting layman seldom thinks of the sermon as an example of artistic production. If it is not 'a part of the ritual', the sermon, he may think, is an unmeditated harangue. Such by misfortune or sheer idleness it may be, particularly in churches where it is customary to lay little stress on the sermon. It is said that John Henry Newman, who had made so great a name for himself as a preacher at Oxford, would later, in his Birmingham days, be suddenly reminded by the opening notes of the organ that he was due to preach, would hurriedly look up the lections for the day and then rush from his study to the pulpit just in time to begin his oration. The story, if true, may explain why succeeding generations have heard so little of the celebrated preacher's Birmingham sermons.

Anglicans, at least, are generally delivered from such haphazard oratory: the sermons to which they are called upon to listen have been as laboriously prepared as they are laboriously read. It remains true, however, that the average layman still prefers what he calls 'extempore' sermons. At least he does not settle down to sleep quite so readily if he does not see a manuscript produced and spread out carefully on the pulpit desk.

Actually, of course, if a preacher does not produce a manuscript, it does not necessarily mean that he has not prepared one. The 'extempore' sermon may be as full of art as the other. Indeed, it may have been written out in its entirety and then committed to memory. In other cases, where the preacher is content to use a few brief notes or a short analysis of what he intends to say, the preparation may well be more exacting than in the case of the full manuscript, for the preacher will go over the subject again and again in thought until the moment when he ascends the pulpit steps.

In spite of the public preference for apparently spontaneous oratory, it should be remembered that grave dangers lie in wait for any speaker who launches himself on this uncharted sea. A very dear colleague of my own, who was much better on the tennis-court than in the pulpit, was once rash enough to devote his discourse to a comparison between the two Greek words for 'good', *kalos* and *agathos*. After spending some minutes becoming more and more entangled in the thickets of his own untrimmed thoughts and finally failing to extricate himself, he summed up by saying, "So you see, my friends, the interesting thing about these two words is that each of them has a meaning different from its own."

In defence of the extemporisers someone may point out that there is a passage in the scriptures which warns us against taking thought for the morrow, and there is another which tells the Christian that when he is brought before a court he must not worry beforehand what he will say, because the right thoughts and words will be given him on the spur of the moment by the Holy Spirit. But this can hardly have been intended, one would have thought, to forbid any kind of preparation of one's discourse. Rather is it meant to inculcate the positive lesson of reliance upon God. And that is not a bad lesson for any public speaker on any occasion.

In either case the sermon, whether written or extempore, must have a form of some sort. Only too many speeches, sacred or secular, remind one of the condition of primordial matter, 'without form and void'. It will be remembered that, according to Genesis, it was the first task of the Spirit to reduce that chaos to some kind of order. The world could not begin to function until the firmaments had been separated, night distinguished from day, and land divided from water.

If such order was necessary in the sphere of divine creation, it is equally necessary in that of the human. Form is essential for anything that would claim the title of art. There can be no art where there is chaos. Art depends for its very being on analysis, division, contrast, composition. That is as true of a painting as of a symphony, of an essay as of a poem. Without form there can be no adequate communication between one human being and another. There is, it seems, a need for some sort of order deep-rooted in the individual soul, and it cries out for satisfaction. Even the most slovenly of housekeepers is not truly happy in a state of hugger-mugger. When it comes to communication, if there is no response to this fundamental need in the spoken or written word, the failure to establish contact is almost complete.

Not quite complete. Sometimes it is the intention of the artist in whatever medium to arouse emotion rather than to start coherent thought, and emotion in its more extreme forms is often both incoherent and inarticulate. Apparently it may be aroused as easily by lack of form as by reasoned exposition. Even so, it would be hazardous to suppose that in such cases form is altogether expendable: beasts and birds have different cries to betoken love or fear. And there is form of a sort even in a woman's scream.

But this consideration really belongs to another part of our subject. All that I wish to establish here is that, properly considered, preaching is an art and may usefully be discussed from that point of view. I once, as you know, even dared in my meditated title, *The Foolishness of Preaching*, to summon St. Paul as a witness for the defence. The phrase (as I have already reminded you) comes from his first Epistle to the Corinthians 1:21, "It has pleased God by the foolishness of preaching to save them that believe." An objection could have been laid against my projected use of the quotation on the ground that the term 'preaching' is ambiguous. Most translators take the original *kerygma* to mean the thing preached rather than the act of preaching, the content rather than the form and delivery of the sermon. We may admit that this is generally so and even cite in support of it chapter 15:14 of the same Epistle: "If Christ be not raised then is my preaching vain (i.e. void of content) and your faith is also vain." But if we turn back to 2:4 of the same Epistle, we find the Apostle saying that his preaching is 'not with persuasive words of man's wisdom', where he is assuredly thinking of the *act* and the way in which it is performed. So we might conceivably feel ourselves justified in asserting that, in the phrase 'foolishness of preaching', the reference is not only to the content of the sermon but also to the manner of its composition and delivery. The foolishness is in the human art, or lack of it, and not in the divine message it conveys. Paul in that case is asking the more sophisticated of his hearers not to be put off by the naive artlessness of his style. Like many another orator, he may have felt that the apology was not really needed, but it made a good point, none the less.

My own point is that we should try to improve our style, as Paul certainly did his. Such at least is the subject of this book. But before we enter upon a detailed discussion of it there is one vitally important matter to be emphasised and kept in memory, both throughout this series of letters and through the whole of the preacher's ministry. That concerns not the form but the content of the preaching.

LETTER 4

Content of Preaching

My dear Robert,

An objection often brought against the consideration of preaching as an art is that emphasis on the form is likely to distract attention from the message delivered. This is true both for the speaker and for the listener. It is quite possible for a preacher to give so much care to the external circumstances and to the literary construction of his sermon that he may neglect the really vital importance of what he has to say. Actually, the form is only the frame to the picture: no good artist would wish so to elaborate his frame as to prevent proper attention being given to the painting itself.

At the same time, the listener may find his attention diverted if the speaker has given too little attention to the external details of his address. Most preachers have been mortified at some time or another at finding interest in what they have been trying to say lost through the emergence of some quite irrelevant and ridiculous incident. An American, who had been disappointed at the lack of rhetoric on the occasion of a 'Quiet Afternoon' for the clergy, remonstrated with the conductor, "There you just sat, and talked to us, and your great fists like hams . . ." Another, after listening to an allocution addressed to a college of preachers, admonished the speaker, "I was interested in your lecture, especially in the way you balanced on that fender as if it were a tightrope. I kept wondering how soon you would fall off."

None of us must allow himself to forget how easy it is for

both speaker and audience to be distracted from the all-important subject-matter by petty and extraneous detail. At the same time, a proper attention to the artistic side of preaching will help the preacher to avoid pitfalls of that kind. In any case it is a paramount duty to do all we possibly can to prevent ourselves from getting in the way of our own message. Let us make no mistake about it; it is the subject-matter that is the truly important thing: beside it the method of presentation is of quite minor significance.

That is what I want to say early in this letter, and to say it so definitely that there will be no later necessity to repeat it. One would be extremely sorry if a discussion devoted to the art of preaching should allow it to be thought that the message to be preached was somehow of less importance than the technique of the preacher. From the theological point of view that is a mere truism, but it should be equally obvious from the pragmatic angle. A preacher who gives his main attention to the manner of his delivery will soon be found to be as hollow as sounding brass or tinkling cymbal. Even worse will be the fate of the preacher who tries to compensate by carefully cultivated voice and gestures for lack of serious thought, whereas a speaker who is really on fire with what he has to say will often carry conviction in spite of uncouth gestures and uncultured voice.

Conviction in the mind of the speaker is, then, the prime necessity. A salesman is not likely to be very successful unless he is convinced that the goods he is trying to sell are *the* goods. The preacher, of all men, must speak out of an honest and good heart. Well then, conviction. But conviction about what? What is the proper content of the Christian sermon? It goes without saying that it must be religious, not artistic or scientific or political, but religious. Now religion, if I may repeat a cliché, is not a thing by itself: it is a way of looking at everything. Religion touches life at so many points that there is almost no limit to what a sermon may contain. But there must be some central and essential core that occurs in every sermon and makes it what it is. Can we find out for ourselves what this distinctive feature must be?

Perhaps our best move would be to go back to our foundation documents and ask what the sermon meant to the New Testament writers. We are told there that both John the Baptist and Jesus himself came preaching the same theme, namely that the Kingdom of God was at hand. That was proclamation and challenge combined. It is perhaps a pity that we do not more often couch our own challenge in the same terms today. The difficulty is that, although there is a sense in which the pronouncement remains eternally true, in the sense then generally taken as original the Kingdom of God did not come in the first century. The notion was in any case a highly technical Jewish conception, which requires a good deal of translation before it can be made to bite into the consciousness of modern man.

Pursuing our enquiries, we are reminded of the sermons that Jesus preached on the Mount and on the Plain, but on investigation we see that these are not sermons in our modern connotation of the term so much as collections of short aphoristic sayings. Beautiful and soul-searching as they are, they do not fall within the categories of the modern sermon, and would not naturally be called by us 'sermons' at all. It is quite possible that originally they were delivered in quite small paragraphs, somewhat like Mao Tse Tung's *Red Book* and were intended to be learnt by heart.

We should be getting nearer to our goal if we examined the sermons attributed to leading apostles in Acts. Even here, however, we should do well not to take them as actual reports of the very words used by the preachers. They are more likely to be specimens of the kind of speeches which the author of Acts thought that the apostles might have delivered in their particular circumstances. They may therefore be even better for our purpose than verbatim reports. They give us an idea of the kind of sermon that church opinion in general would have thought proper in such circumstances.

Here then is the outline of a sermon by St. Peter to the Pentecost congregation after the descent of the Holy Spirit (Acts 2:14–39):

1. What you see around you is evidence that God's long-promised plan for the world has been fulfilled.
2. Jesus was the chosen instrument, but you crucified him.
3. Nevertheless the situation was retrieved by his resurrection and ascension, as had been foretold in Scripture.
4. This then is the challenge to you: Believe in him; repent and be baptized.

Here is Peter again, this time talking to Gentiles (10:34–43):

1. God has no favourites.
2. He sent the good news of peace to all through Jesus Christ;
3. Who was crucified but was raised to life again.
4. And has been designated by God as judge of quick and dead.
5. All who trust in him receive forgiveness of sins.

As an example of Paul's preaching, we may take his sermon to a mixed congregation of Jews and proselytes in the synagogue at Pisidian Antioch (13:17–41):

1. God's dealings with Israel down to the times of David, of whose posterity Jesus was born.
2. His unique mission was heralded by John the Baptist.
3. Jesus was crucified through a gross misunderstanding on the part of the Jews.
4. He was buried but was raised again and appeared frequently to his friends.
5. This was all part of God's age-old plan to bring forgiveness and salvation to the world.

6. You must take this warning, and escape the doom proclaimed by the prophets against all who oppose God's word.

These outlines can be compared with other sermons recorded in Acts, but the general tenor will be found to be the same: human life can only be explained on the ground that God always has had a plan for man's ultimate happiness and salvation; this plan was adumbrated in the history of the Jewish people, but was brought to its great climacteric in the life and work of Jesus of Nazareth; he was executed as a common criminal, but was raised from the dead, and in his exalted condition is to be the judge of all mankind; if you wish to escape condemnation you must take advantage of this plan, repent of your sins and give your whole-hearted allegiance to him.

We may take it, then, that this is the 'message' of Christianity as conceived by its first preachers: God's plan, its implementation in the life, death and resurrection of Jesus; and the coming moral judgment for all mankind. This should be a brief enough summary in all conscience. But if we are thorough Paulines and wish to narrow it down still further, we can recall how he said that there was only one thing on which he would wish to pride himself, and that was the cross of our Lord Jesus Christ, "by whom the world was crucified unto me and I unto the world" (Gal. 6:14). And this, he claimed in another letter, was the sole subject of his preaching, at least while he was with the Corinthians (1 Cor. 2:2).

Why a gallows should be regarded as the one thing worth thinking and speaking about is not immediately obvious to the outsider, or even perhaps to the initiate; but at least the latter knows that it is the symbol of hope for the world, and the former may be glad of an opportunity to have the mystery explained at least once.

But there is the rub. It may be said with some justification that, although this kind of preaching may have been exciting enough while it was still news, after two thousand years of proclamation it has become dull, and exercises a naturally soporific effect upon the hearer. Here lies the main difficulty of the preacher's profession. To make long-past history come alive in the present; to make what was significant to humanity in its youth seem equally vital in what it fondly believes is its maturity; to make long-familiar phrases of prose or poetry awake the 'first fine careless rapture' and set the listener on fire with determination: all that demands a power of communication of the very highest order. No wonder that Christians throughout the ages have seen in it a special gift of the Holy Spirit.

Only one thing can warrant such an effort, and that is the profound conviction that what one has to say is the most important thing in the world, and that it can, and will, make all the difference in men's lives. What the preacher has to talk about is not just a matter of history: the Christ still lives in the present. The acts of God are not just done and done with: they belong to eternity; their significance reverberates through the corridors of time and they have their impact today upon each believer just as they had in the first moment of their happening.

As the preacher looks down from his pulpit at the congregation in the pews, he must believe with all his heart that this may prove true in the case of each individual among them. Even if they are already what is called 'converted', or, to use a modern term, 'committed', the realisation of it should be renewed from Sunday to Sunday and indeed from day to day. It is true that the feeling may not be so vivid as on the first occasion—man's psychological reactions are too varied and uncertain for that—but the knowledge and recognition should be there, and may be fanned at any moment into fresh flame through the obvious sincerity of the preacher.

It is clear, however, that the preacher's own psychological reactions must be subject to the same variations as those of the congregation. He cannot always be on fire with his message: he too has his moments of recession. Nor is it wise to feign what he does not feel. Any attempt to work himself up into a state of excitation, however unconscious it may be, will soon be discovered and condemned as hypocritical. It used to be said of a very emotive politician that in his speeches he always believed what he said 'while he was saying it'. Nowadays television is supposed to be a ruthless revealer of oratorical duplicity. In any case, for the preacher, above all men, sincerity is of the very essence. Consequently he learns to rely, not upon the emotions of the moment, but upon the steady, underlying consciousness of what his conviction really is. It is that conviction which by the grace of God he must communicate to others.

'By the grace of God': that after all is the secret. The Christian priest or minister believes that the Spirit of God is with him while he speaks in God's name. Hence the solemn invocation and ascription with which he begins and ends his sermon. They imply that this is no ordinary oration, but a word spoken by God's messenger to God's people in the power of God's own Spirit.

Of this essential condition I may have more to say in another letter, but in the meantime I cannot do better than repeat the wise advice given by a very experienced preacher to young men who are just learning the trade:

What is the rule then? It is: be natural; forget yourself; be so absorbed in what you are doing and in the realisation of the presence of God, and in the glory and greatness of the Truth that you are preaching, and the occasion that brings you together that you are so taken up by all this that you forget yourself completely. That is the right condition; that is the only place of safety; that is the only way in which you can honour God. Self is the greatest enemy of the preacher, more so than in the case of any other man in society. And the only

way to deal with self is to be so taken up with, and so en-
raptured by, the glory of what you are doing, that you forget
yourself altogether. D. M. Lloyd-Jones, *Preaching and
Preachers*, p. 264.

Categories of Sermons

My dear Robert,

From the high level at which I concluded my last letter it may seem a somewhat steep descent to embark upon a consideration of the main types into which sermons must fall. Yet it is a quite essential task for the preacher. If he has only one message to proclaim, it nevertheless applies to so many situations that the variety of possible presentation is almost endless. The preacher's range of choice is at least as wide as that of the journalist. For the moment we intend to consider no more than the main types. Three stand out clearly.

It is C. H. Dodd who in this country has taught us to distinguish most sharply between *kerygma* and *didache*, proclamation and teaching. His view is that there always was a line of demarcation between the proclamation of the good news, which was intended to challenge and convert, and the teaching, which was intended to give instruction to the convert in Christian belief and practice. A similar distinction was familiar in Judaism between the functions of prophet and rabbi; but in Christianity both functions seem to have been exercised often by the same individual. This custom has led later ages to confuse the two categories. Certainly it might be said that in practice we have hardly tried to keep the two varieties apart. Nevertheless, even if it is a mistake for the preacher to try to keep them in watertight compartments, it is well for him to hold the difference always in mind, so that he may have clearly before him the effect at which he aims in any particular sermon.

It is probable that we ought to find room in addition to these two for a third main category, that of the liturgical sermon. This type is meant to be above all an aid to devotion. If the proclamation appeals mostly to the will and the instruction mainly to the intellect, the devotional will appeal above all to the emotions. But it must be emphasised again, as in the case of the other two, that the liturgical sermon need not, and does not, keep strictly within its own precise limits. Both proclamation and instruction are expected to lead to devotion, while devotion, if it has no adequate support in will and reason, can hardly escape the danger of becoming mere superstition.

At a later stage we may consider each of these categories in some detail. But already it is time that we give them at least a cursory glance; otherwise, when we come to analyse specific elements of preaching we shall be at the disadvantage of not understanding what in any instance is the preacher's general aim. That is a fault all too common, not only among the preachers themselves, but also among their critics.

I

In a proclamation-type sermon the preacher sets himself the task of announcing the good news of salvation. So long as this was really news, there was no doubt about people listening to it, whether they received it with acceptance or derision. Today, because the newness has worn off, the preacher must recognise that he has to begin by attracting attention. Every experienced speaker knows well what a difference it makes to the attention of his audience if there is already a thrill in the air. On the occasion of some national disaster or even of some local festivity, there is already a lively awareness making itself felt, and the speaker has merely to put himself *en rapport* with his hearers to avoid losing it. It is this atmosphere of expectancy that gives a tremendous advantage to a bishop or other 'occasional' preacher.

The situation is likely to be entirely different if one is a familiar figure in a local pulpit and there has been nothing to set the congregation agog. If anyone is to stab the audience broad awake, it must be the preacher himself. He will therefore give special attention to his opening words, for with them the battle may be won or lost. Northcliff used to advise his young journalists to make their point in the first two lines of their story. "If you don't get your reader's attention then, you won't get it at all, because he won't bother to read the rest." The old maxim that an essayist should keep his *bonne bouche* for the end is no longer recommended. A journalist has been known to say that he spent half his time trying to avoid the temptation to write a resounding curtain-line. But I think he was wrong.

The preacher of the proclamation-type sermon may be helped to get into the right mood if he remembers that he is still today dealing with a live situation. In the middle of the last century the missionary was obviously needed in darkest Africa, because what he had to say would there be regarded as amazing news. Today, the missionary is needed in darkest England. If there are not many avowed heathen in his congregation, there will certainly be a proportion who do not consider themselves to be committed Christians. Somehow the age-old story must be made to sound in their ears with the sharp tones of a peremptory challenge.

Not that the gauntlet is to be thrown down without sympathy for the challenged. Any suspicion of *de haut en bas* will destroy the possibility of sympathy between speaker and audience, and the hearer who is hovering between loneliness and despair will be plunged into even greater misery. If the speaker's message is to be one of divine love, the revelation must be conveyed in the sympathy of his whole attitude no less than in his precise words.

II

In turning from preaching as proclamation to preaching as instruction, we naturally ask whether we still have Jesus as our exemplar. Scholars sometimes debate whether we ought to picture him as a prophet haranguing the crowds from a hill and a boat, or whether we should see him as a typical rabbi of his day seated with his disciples around him, engaged in a serious game of question and answer and dictating the maxims he would have them learn by rote.

The answer is that assuredly we must have both pictures constantly before our eyes, and should model our own preaching on both. Certainly we must not exclude instruction. The preacher who confined his sermons to proclaiming the need for conversion would become wearisome to a degree, particularly if he preached to the same congregation Sunday by Sunday. Further, he would deny his people an important support for their faith, if he did not keep them well informed in Christian doctrine and practice. True, methods of teaching have changed. We no longer place much emphasis on learning by heart (although in some subjects it will never cease to be necessary). Nowadays we prefer to accompany our pupils on a voyage of enquiry, because we think that what they discover for themselves will form a more permanent part of their intellectual equipment as well as provide a better form of training.

The main difficulty about a teaching sermon lies in the composition of the congregation, comprising, as it does, members of all ages and of all stages of culture. How can one treat a subject attractively and effectively for the benefit of so varied a body of learners? Surely not by being donnish or pedantic, but by being as simple and natural as possible, and by assuming from the outset that we have something to say worth hearing and that the people really do want to know what it is.

A further difficulty is that in our generation the parson has to a large extent lost his position as an instructor. At least, before he is accepted as such he must in each individual case prove his claim to the title. He is no longer the representative of learning among the unlearned. The old aphorism that the privileged classes must educate their masters has been put into effect, and the parson now may find himself less advanced in general knowledge than a considerable proportion of his flock. As for specialised knowledge, advances in several sciences have been so rapid that even the boys and girls in his own parochial schools may well be ahead of him.

In such circumstances what is the preacher to do? I suggest that the shoemaker should stick to his last. While he may draw upon his total experience of life for his illustrations, the substance of his sermons should be confined to his own particular field. There is one subject in which he is certain to be well ahead of his congregation, and that is theology. I often wonder why more of the clergy do not make use of their specialised knowledge. Perhaps it is because here at least the preacher has a proper standard of judgment. He knows enough to realise how technical is his subject, how rapidly it advances, and how far he himself lags behind the professional theologian. Sheer modesty prevents him from posing as an authority in a field in which he is only too well aware of his shortcomings.

It is all too likely that those textbooks he so laboriously analysed at college have been sold off to the second-hand dealer, or auctioned off to his classmates. The lecture-notes he so carefully took down, and even the essays in which he compressed, for the benefit of his tutor, such knowledge as he had acquired have been consigned to the waste-paper basket or thrown upon the garden bonfire. How foolish! There, if he had only recognised the fact, lay the theological basis of his whole ministry. Those books and notes should have been the tools of his trade. No priest or pastor can function adequately without such an equipment. Very few people can carry all necessary knowledge in their heads: most soon come to realise that the important matter is not to know a fact but to know where it can be found. Of course, one admits without hestitation that the preacher has to instruct not in theology but in religion; but theology is only 'thinking about religion', or at least about God, and if you want to set your congregation to thinking about religion it is just as well to be able to direct them along ways already traversed by admitted experts.

The preacher's task is to make theology come alive for his congregation. He need not fear that they must necessarily find it monotonous or dull; its scope is too vast for that. The last time I counted up in a respectable encyclopedia the various branches of theology, there were no less than twenty-four of them: that was a long time ago and a few more have been added since then. The subject covers far too much of human and divine life ever to be intrinsically dull. In any case, people are generally ready to listen to a man talking about his own job. It is to be presumed that there, at least, he knows what he is talking about; and it is always interesting even for the un-committed layman to see how the other half of the world thinks.

III

When we come to consider the devotional type of preaching, it is more necessary than ever to remember that these types of sermon are not watertight compartments. Devotion must enter into every sermon of whatever type; any sermon that does not lead to devotion is lost. At the same time there should be room for sermons wholly assigned to this subject: they do not aim primarily at converting the unconverted or at strengthening their intellectual grasp of the faith, but they do aim at carrying the thoughts of the congregation directly up to God and main-taining them there.

Here again we have Jesus as our pattern. "Teach us to pray," said his disciples, and he not only gave them instruction on how

c   33

to pray, but also provided them with a sample prayer which has been used as a model and formed a link between God and man ever since. It is a curious thing that, in spite of this explicit response, the followers of Jesus have been making the same request from his day to our own. "Teach us to pray" is by far the most frequent request on the lips of enquirers. That is sure evidence of a hunger that is always there and is never completely satisfied. There is always a demand for a truly devotional sermon.

Since the very object of such a discourse must be to bring people into the felt presence of God, it is necessary here, even more than on other occasions, to create and preserve a genuinely 'numinous' atmosphere. This cannot be done by any meretricious aping of devotion: the preacher's insincerity would be at once detected and his effort would fail. He must begin by placing himself deliberately and whole-heartedly in the presence of God, and he must pray that by no untoward word or gesture or tone of voice may he prevent his people from full awareness of that presence. He must never allow his own personality to obtrude itself between God and his people. The way to avoid that danger is to be completely absorbed in the thought of God himself.

The purpose, then, of the preacher in this instance is not to challenge or instruct, but to create a mood or attitude of mind. To achieve this aim he must have some point from which to begin. As we have already seen, circumstances may already have given him his point of departure; some local or national event may have already set the mood of expectation. If not, he may find his emotional starting-point in something that has happened in the service: a psalm, a hymn, a passage from the lessons, a phrase from the liturgy, the striking words of his text, or it may be the feast of the day leading to a paean of thanksgiving. The presence of God is found, and that sets the tone of the whole discourse.

I may have more to say about the devotional sermon in a later letter, when we come to discuss the liturgical homily specifically. In the meantime I wonder whether you have ever come across the categories of sermons listed by W. E. Sangster,* the well-known Methodist preacher. He was accustomed to divide sermons into no less than six classes: Biblical, Devotional (ethical), Doctrinal, Apologetic (philosophical), Social, and Evangelistic. It would be a good exercise for you as a beginner, before going further, to see how these six fit into our smaller list of three.

* Horton Davies, *Varieties of English Preaching*, p. 209 (S.C.M., 1963).

Structure of the Sermon

My dear Robert,

The point to be discussed in this letter is how a sermon is built up. I must say at the outset that you ought not to expect from me anything elaborate or recherché, because that would destroy my whole idea of the way in which the thing ought to be done. If one reads of the methods pursued by the medieval and reformation preachers, one is amazed at the complications in which they apparently delighted to become involved. But then, of course, their sermons lasted for a very long time and therefore demanded many divisions and sub-divisions. Today, with our much shorter discourses, such elaboration would be entirely out of place; the main effort of the preacher nowadays should be devoted to keeping himself as simple as possible.

The reason is that the congregation has almost no visible aid to assist it in following the sermon: apart from their view of the preacher, the listeners must trust to their sense of hearing alone. If they are to ponder it and keep it in memory, the plan must be as plain as possible. Memory depends largely upon visualisation, and, for clear visualisation without material aids, simplicity is thoroughly essential. (Of course you realise that you can 'visualise' something mentally without actually seeing it physically.)

It goes almost without saying that if this is true for the congregation, it is even more true for the preacher. If he is what is called an 'extemporary' preacher, he must be able to see his whole discourse before him at once, just as Mozart is said to have seen his sonatas. To see a speech steadily and to see it whole, plainness of structure is the greatest help. One knows from bitter experience how seldom a complicated scheme comes off. Even if the speaker himself does not become confused, his audience most certainly will. They cannot picture his outline, and they therefore lose the thread of his argument—or of his several arguments.

Even if he uses a manuscript he will be happier, in my opinion, if he keeps his outline simple. It requires a professional essayist with plenty of room to spare to follow an intricate scheme without giving the impression of rambling. The canvas of an ordinary modern sermon is much too small to allow of much conglomeration.

In this connection an interesting question arises: whether the speaker should reveal his outline. Normally, platform speakers do not do so for fear they should rouse ridicule by aping the method of the preacher, 'firstly, secondly, thirdly,' and so on. Perhaps if the more woolly speakers had the courage to do it, they would begin to realise how few points they had to make. Even if it is not necessary for the preacher, it may be very helpful for the congregation to be given some indication of the course he proposes to follow. At least they will know that they are getting somewhere. My own view, for what it is worth, is that a preacher does well to show his hand occasionally, but not so often as to let the method become stale, soporific, or ridiculous.

No doubt the situation is altered in churches where the preacher's enumeration is regarded as a directive for others taking part in the service. Once in the great church of St. Ouen in Rouen I stood among the red-robed choristers gathered at the pulpit steps to listen to the sermon. The preacher was long and prosy, and the boys were getting restless. At last he said, '*Enfin*'. Immediately the boys were nudging each other in the ribs, repeating '*Enfin, enfin*', and ran off to take their place in choir before the peroration was over. Did not Shakespeare sometimes use rhymes in his plays to give notice of the termination of an act? Perhaps modern organists, vergers and sidesmen are not so ready to take a cue from the pulpit, but even they might be helped if they could tell when the sermon had almost run its course.

I

Leaving these preliminary considerations on one side, we come to the more important discussion of varieties of structure. The first outline to which nostalgia demands some reference is the one to which I was most accustomed in my youth. It had three divisions: an exposition of the text (including its context); an explanation of the doctrine arising from it; and an explication of the ethics or actual conduct demanded by that doctrine.

This was a very simple and satisfactory outline, consisting merely of text, teaching and practice, or of context, creed and conduct. It included all that was essential, but if the novice found it not sufficiently detailed and was afraid of running out of matter, each division was capable of almost infinite sub-division. It could be adapted to any one of the three types of preaching already described — challenge, instruction, devotion — but was in fact most easily associated with the type of preaching known as 'expository'. It had plenty of backing in the New Testament and was, in fact, the kind of framework on which St. Paul built a number of his epistles.

Its disadvantage was that it was almost fatally easy: it lent itself to endless repetition and could thus become dreadfully dull. Many preachers would write their sermons carefully enough in the first instance, but would then store them away for use when the next appropriate Sunday came round. The discourses were not likely on their second or third appearance to be recognised, unless the preacher had introduced some story or illustrative matter which had caught the attention of his hearers. Stories are good, but they have an unfortunate habit of lingering in the memory long after the point that gave rise to them has been forgotten. However, the stories were not numerous, because quite a lot of preachers at that time seemed to have a conscientious objection to making their sermons interesting. No doubt they were afraid of appearing frivolous.

Nevertheless, it would not be fair to write in too deprecatory a spirit about the nineteenth-century tractarian sermon. It contained much very conscientious teaching, and in the hand (or mouth) of a John Henry Newman could attain a rare level of eloquence and solemnity. In general it was sound, steady, and sincere. Before we decry it as being 'thoroughly Victorian' we ought to be very sure that we have something better with which to replace it.

II

Actually, what we have done in our day is to settle down to an even more stereotyped structure. An introduction, three points and a conclusion have become so common a pattern as to be almost derisory. Yet we should make a great mistake if we let ourselves be laughed out of it. In any case, if we are ashamed of its naivety, we can easily escape any actual mention of its divisions, although it is sometimes good to let the congregation see them, not only for the sake of clarity, upon which we have already agreed, but also as an *aide mémoire*.

As for the divisions themselves, they disclose their character in their names. The introduction serves the same purpose as the overture to an opera: it reveals the point of the whole theme, and should be attractive enough to arouse curiosity as to how it is later to be developed. This introductory statement may be made very shortly or at some length. While we are young we are probably glad to use it as a sub-section to fill out a discourse which otherwise we fear is going to be rather meagre. As we grow older and more loquacious, we have to restrain ourselves in order to keep it in proper proportion to the main body of the sermon. Sometimes a mere sentence is enough: "This morning I am going to talk about . . .", and then one plunges *in medias res*.

When it is as short as that, the introduction really performs the same service for a speaker as does his title for a writer. Personally, whichever trade I happen to be following at the moment, I never dispense with a title. If I am writing an article for a paper, I put a title at the top of it, although I know that some sub-editor is likely to scrap it or reshape it when it comes his way. It is still useful to me, because it compels me to realise that I am writing about some special thing, and it forces me to state that something in the shortest and most precise terms possible, which is good exercise for any writer. But I still do the same if for the moment I am a speaker. Even if the written preparation of my speech or sermon is confined to half a sheet of notepaper, and even if I don't put pen to paper at all but keep the whole thing in my head, I still want a title: it will ensure that there is at least one point in what I mean to say.

In any case, we must not let the introduction become too long, otherwise we may never arrive at the detailed analysis of our theme, and the introduction will be like a porch to a house that does not exist. Once in an Irish college I was shown a splendid façade, and was told that it was the library. "How lovely," I said. "May we go in?" "Oh, no," I was told. "You can't go in: that is only the door. We shall build the library when we have collected the money." One hears too many sermons that turn out to be like that library.

When we get to the main theme, we divide it into three points. Everything goes in threes: it is a good natural number and easy to remember. It is said that even monkeys can count up to three but become hopelessly confused if their hunters take a fourth man. No doubt speakers with a gift of fluency can do with fewer than three points, but those who, like myself, find both ideas and words hard to come by, often divide the sections each into three sub-sections. These should all follow logically one upon another. "It is the 'wherefores' and the 'therefores' you have to watch", as a reliable expert was wont to say. No doubt such logical conjunctives are out of fashion today, and it is perhaps better if they are not too frequently expressed, but they surely must be there in the mind of the speaker. With this aid, uttered or unexpressed, he can with comparative ease learn to picture a whole speech without ever putting pen to paper.

If one is not logic-conscious, memorising a train of thought may be much more difficult. A way of doing it is to contrive that the initial letters of each sub-section join together to form a name or well-known combination of capitals by which so many institutions nowadays recognise themselves. The cleverest of such *aides-mémoire* I have ever come across was in the lecture of a professor from Louvain. He began by asking twenty members of his audience, taken at haphazard, to say each in succession the word that first came into his head. At the conclusion of his full hour's talk he repeated with complete accuracy, so far as we could tell, the list of unrelated and nonsensical words. When asked how he did it, he said that he always had in mind the story of Adam and Eve and fitted into it the words as they were said. All he had to do afterwards was to unroll the story and the words came tumbling out. I admit that he was a professor of psychology and his method may be less easy for the amateur, but his experiment at least showed how much can be done by the use of suitable mnemonics. Only one caution must be added: don't let the mnemonic get too elaborate or it may be more easily forgotten than the points you wish to memorise.

If I seem to be talking as if all preaching was extemporary, that only means that I am talking out of personal experience. I do not think I have read a manuscript from the pulpit more than once or twice in the whole course of sixty-six years in the ordained ministry, though I have often envied the people who do. We may have an opportunity later to say something about the relative merits of the written and the spoken sermon. In the meantime let us return to our study of the structure of the discourse, whether written or not.

III

One of the most attractive methods of constructing a discourse, though one not widely applicable, is to take two contrasting ideas and to balance them against each other at several different levels. If examples of the other methods hitherto considered can be found in St. Paul, this one is practically common form with St. John. He takes such ideas as light and darkness, life and death, flesh and spirit, and uses the apparent contradiction between them to bring out his most telling lessons.

A modern example of structure by means of developing contrast is to be found in a recent newspaper sermon* by Bishop F. R. Barry. His text is verse 45 of the 119th Psalm: "I will walk at liberty, for I seek thy commandments." He begins by asking whether there is not an implied contradiction in the use side by side of the terms 'liberty' and 'commandments'. Mill's definition of liberty as 'freedom to do what one desires' seems to be at complete variance with the note of obligation suggested by a moral law with its notion of 'ought'. The preacher considers this logical contradiction at the level of morals. The common notion, he says, that freedom is directly opposed to a moral code is utterly negatived by Kant's conception of that 'categorical imperative' without which man cannot be a human being at all. But that does not mean that an absolute moral law decides man's proper conduct in every possible situation even before it occurs. The norm states the principle, which must then be interpreted in accordance with circumstances as they arise. Man's freedom lies in his capacity to choose the principles by which he will be guided.

* *The Times*, July 8th, 1972.

The discussion next moves to the political sphere. It is pointed out that what is adumbrated in the text is not a political but a religious freedom, the freedom to become what God wants us to be. This, however, does not release us from the need for some measure of political freedom. For instance, an omnicompetent State can, if it neglects its housing, education and general welfare, prevent people from attaining their proper physical, mental and spiritual development. It is therefore significant that today the question is being hotly debated how far the State is responsible for protecting its subjects from moral contamination.

Finally the preacher asks what is the solution of the problem raised by this apparent contradiction. Dr. Barry answers that permissiveness, laissez-faire, is no substitute for true liberty. The only solution is a 'trans-political' freedom. What is needed is a supernatural allegiance which will bring all social programmes under criticism in accordance with the Christian valuation of man.

This, you will think, is a sermon for the élite. It is nevertheless a model of its type, and can be imitated in the working out of a simpler theme.

IV

You may deem it an ill-timed pleasantry if I go on to suggest that another possible structure for the sermon is a circular one. Yet, after all, there is a good deal to be said for talking in circles, so long as you remember on each occasion to close the circle and finish up on the note from which you started. A text is not well used as a mere point of departure. Its end is in its beginning. We treat it best if, after we have used it as the basis of a logical argument, merely to repeat it seems an adequate and proper way to conclude the sermon. If we seek New Testament examples, we can find a notable adaptation of it once again in St. John, whose writings are largely made up of a series of small

43

circles in which he keeps going back to the same word or idea. Each circle, however, conveys some fresh light on his theme, and so he achieves a kind of spiral effect in which each circle takes him a little higher. I have heard a present-day preacher do the same thing with great effect in a kind of meditative monologue in which the same word or phrase was repeated with a regularity that would have proved monotonous if the spiritual thought conveyed had not been so intensely moving.

A specific example of this type can be found in the sermon inserted by St. Paul into his second letter to the Corinthians (chapters 8 and 9). It is the more striking as it is concerned with the most distasteful of all subjects on which the preacher has to exercise his art, namely the raising of money. The Apostle says he is going to talk about generosity, the generosity which is a God-given grace. That virtue has been recently shown, he says, in a marked degree by the congregations in Macedonia. "Now," he continues, "we expect it to be displayed by you; and that is why we have sent Titus to you. We know from the outset that you will remember the example of the Lord Jesus, who, although he was rich, yet for your sake became poor, so that through his poverty you might become rich. This was generosity indeed. What I am now asking of my readers is something quite reasonable. To exercise the grace of generosity is good even for themselves, for they may one day need the service which they are now asked to render to Christians elsewhere. In any case, what God cares about is not the amount they give, but the spirit in which they give it. Generosity must be displayed generously, so that as far as possible everyone may have an equal chance of sharing God's bounty. To put this in order, we are sending along with Titus (whom we warmly commend to your kindness) certain officially appointed delegates. It will be good for them to see that our pride in you was justified: don't let us down: remember that niggardly sowing involves niggardly reaping. Let everyone see that your generosity is really a grace given by God."

We cannot help noticing how closely St. Paul has stuck to his text all through: generosity, collection, example of Jesus, collection, generosity: that, no doubt, is why there is no sense of incongruity when he openly returns to it at the end. There seems no reason why the method should not be followed today. It always gives a congregation a happy feeling to find a preacher ending up where he began. The reminiscence of his opening theme may be marked by the repetition of a phrase, or suggested by the overtones of a single word, used in the beginning; or it may be conveyed by a brief sentence summing up the whole argument, or even by the mere iteration of his text. In any case the congregation is not only reminded of the main point he has been trying to emphasise, but he also has the comforting assurance that he knew all the time what he wanted to say and that he has triumphantly brought to conclusion a well-thought-out plan. Such treatment produces a feeling of confidence towards the preacher, which may turn out valuable in many other departments of parochial and pastoral life.

It will be noticed that I do not share the journalist's dislike of a 'hard finish' to his article. Perhaps it is not so important for him as for the preacher. After all, his reader has got it all down in print, and when he has read the story he can always turn back to the beginning if he wants to pick up a point. But the listener has no such opportunity. He must be reminded of the beginning by what is said at the end, or, as likely as not, he will have lost it for ever.

Forgive me for this rather long letter. But it really is important that we should realise how flexible is the structure of a sermon. It will be a help to you as well as to your congregation, and spare you both a good deal of boredom, if you can ring a number of changes and so impart an element of variety into your compositions. In any case I can't guarantee that my letters won't be even longer in future.

45

LETTER 7

Manuscript or Extempore?

My dear Robert,

The first and perhaps most difficult question with which a
novice in the preacher's art is faced is whether he shall read a
manuscript or speak without a note. This is to put the problem
in its most extreme form: very few preachers appear in the
pulpit without a paper of some sort. There are many inter-
mediate choices, such as the use of notes, either full or sparse,
and the writing of a sermon in full, which is then committed to
memory, so that the manuscript may be discarded in the pulpit.
The problem thus becomes one of the nicely calculated less or
more. Of one thing we may be certain: that there is never such
a thing (except in totally unexpected circumstances) as a truly
extemporary sermon, that is to say one that is thought up and
delivered on the spur of the moment.

This may seem an odd confession to make on behalf of the
representatives of one who said, "Be not anxious beforehand
what ye shall speak: but whatsoever shall be given you in that
hour, that speak ye: for it is not ye that speak, but the Holy
Ghost." (Mark 13:11) It must be remembered, however, that
this injunction does not apply directly to the preaching of the
gospel but to an appearance in court after the gospel had been
preached. Dennis Nineham's note on this passage is particularly
sympathetic: "When we remember that most of the early
Christians were simple and unlearned people, for whom a
speech in court would have been a terrible ordeal, we realise
how much such a promise will have meant to them." (Pelican
St. Mark, p. 349)

46

The general consensus of Christian opinion all down the centuries has been that the proclamation of the gospel demands the utmost care that can be given it. Such premeditation does not exclude the influence of the Holy Spirit, but serves as the dedicated instrument of his intervention. The 'charismatic' gift of the Holy Spirit may surely apply as much to the preparation of the sermon as to its presentation.

In regarding the written sermon as the norm, one is thinking mainly of English practice. In this country we may very well have gone too far in leaving the delivery of the unwritten word to the street corner, Hyde Park and Tower Hill. Within the consecrated building, particularly in the cathedral, many a preacher would regard it as almost indecent to enter the pulpit without a manuscript. Indeed this convention sometimes occasions the raising of an eyebrow in circles outside the Establishment. One remembers from one's boyhood the furore that arose over Durham Cathedral's failure to provide a sermon on the morning when the scheduled preacher missed his train. The press speedily added up the princely stipends received by the canons, and the local pastors said, "All that money, and not one of them could say a word for Christ." One of the canons of Salisbury was so shattered by this vicarious experience that ever afterwards he kept a spare sermon in his stall, together with his voice-lozenges and a spare half-crown in case he forgot his collection money.

In any event, the choice may not be quite so wide open for the budding preacher as we might suppose. There is always the preliminary question whether he is capable of dispensing with a manuscript even if he wishes. It is a matter not so much of the capacity to improvise thoughts as of the ability to clothe them in suitable words on the spur of the moment. Some would-be speakers, and among them often the most intelligent, find that the power to string words together, to form them into sentences, and to keep the sentences a coherent whole disappears altogether as soon as they rise to their feet and face an expectant audience. It is strange how many writers, such as journalists, novelists, scholars, turn out to be bad extempore speakers. Perhaps it is because, when they use their pen or their typewriter, they can put together words at their own leisure, whereas in speaking they have no time to stop and think things over.

It is not possible to burke this question altogether, and it is better to face up to it from the beginning. Even if you are blest with an exceptional memory and can, without too much difficulty, commit to it a laboriously written manuscript, it is almost certain that at some point or other the precise form of words will escape you. Then, without some capacity to improvise, you will be lost. That is what happened once to Bishop Gore when, in the middle of a quotation from Browning, he forgot his lines. It is said that he was so shaken by the experience that he could not resume his discourse, and had to descend from the pulpit with his sermon unfinished.

Fortunately one has known instances where the outcome has been happier. I attended as chaplain in my young days the Bishop of Peterborough, Dr. Blagden, at his enthronement. I noticed that he seemed worried as I led him to the pulpit, but he settled down and preached a beautiful sermon. Afterwards, in the vestry, I asked him what was the matter. He replied, "My manuscript; I couldn't find it anywhere. It has only just turned up in the leaves of my Bible." Thirty years later, as Bishop of London, I had to attend a very distinguished judge when he opened the post-war repair work to the Old Bailey. He began reading a manuscript but after the first sentence or two threw it down and proceeded without a note to deliver an eloquent and important oration. Afterwards in the robing-room he had some very pointed remarks to make about the television people. "They had their cameras straight in my eyes, and I could not see a word."

I am still lost in admiration of these two men for the smoothness with which they were able to effect the transition from one style of speaking to another. Certainly I could not have done it myself. I have several times been called upon by misadventure to deliver without a moment's notice what should have been an important speech or sermon, and I have managed somehow to get by. But then I had not been relying on some manuscript which was unexpectedly snatched from my use. It is much easier to maintain your stance if you have not been leaning on some prop which is suddenly plucked away from you.

The point I am trying to establish is that any speaker, before he dispenses with his script, must make sure that he can talk coherently without one. If this sounds rather like warning a boy not to go near the water until he has learnt to swim, one can reply that anyone who desires to become a preacher, or indeed a public speaker of any kind, should take every opportunity of learning how to do it before he is put to the test. Debating societies at school, college, and university are the best training-grounds, though organisations like the Church Army and the College of Preachers have their own specialised methods. On this head, by the way, it might be illuminating to find out how many of the modern Archbishops of Canterbury had in their earlier days been president of their University Union.

In his training period the would-be speaker has to develop a fairly thick skin. He will often find his audience bored and sometimes contemptuous, but he must push on relentlessly. After all, he has to learn his job. This cannot be done without experience, and experience can only be gained through experiments on living victims. It is not until he knows what extempore speaking feels like that the learner will be able to decide for himself what his attitude towards the use of a manuscript on his own part shall be. To decide that issue he will perhaps wish to sum up the pros and cons on either side.

To begin on the scriptless side. As I have already suggested, most laymen, at least of the less intellectual type, seem to prefer their preacher to dispense with a manuscript. They feel that, as listeners, they keep in much more vital contact with a preacher who has no need to rivet his eyes on the written page all the time. They also feel, wrongly, that the spontaneous preacher speaks with the greater sincerity. The unsophisticated listener is more than usually naive in this view. Apparent spontaneity is no evidence of sincerity. The most eloquent speaker I ever heard was the late Earl of Rosebery. It was early in the present century, and he was unveiling a bust of Mr. Gladstone in the Oxford Union. It was a speech whose oratory fitted the occasion. Towards the end it mounted towards a great climax of excitement in which the arms, body and voice of the speaker all united to draw the audience into a surge of emotion. It was most effective, but even I, comparatively inexperienced as I was, could see behind the scenes sufficiently to sense that the whipping up of the tension was deliberate. I do not for one moment believe that the speaker was insincere, but I felt sure that, although he read no manuscript, the expression of his enthusiasm was carefully designed and rehearsed. If we wish to judge a speaker's sincerity, we must certainly find some other criterion than the presence or absence of a script.

I should like to note in passing that this attribute of sincerity is capable of much finer distinctions than are generally allowed. Every speaker must be conscious at some time or other of an inner voice asking him, even in the full flight of some rhetorical passage, "Am I being really sincere about this or am I just putting on an act for the benefit of the hearers?" Such tendency to introspection even in the middle of a tense moment, when one would have thought that the totality of his psychological resources were concentrated on the objective task in hand, can be most disconcerting to any speaker, but most of all to the man in the pulpit. The more serious he is, the more disturbing it may be. What is he to do? He certainly cannot stop and argue the point with himself then and there. I suggest that he should stop asking himself what he is feeling at the moment and fall back upon the steady attitude of mind that was his before he began making this particular speech. He can settle accounts with himself later. In any case, is there not something in the Scriptures about leaving such matters to God "who is greater than our heart and knoweth all things"? (1 John 3:10)

It is the fear of such hidden struggles that makes many preachers keep the emotional tone of their discourses deliberately low. Liddon, when he was preaching at St. Paul's, always read the more emotional passages of his sermons, but discarded his manuscript for the rest. This was surely carrying caution a little too far, unless indeed he was afraid of his own eloquence and feared that his zeal might carry him over the bound of propriety. If he had been a platform speaker he might well have feared that the responsive enthusiasm of his audience might impel him to say things for which he would afterwards be sorry. Nevertheless, in spite of all these difficulties, it remains true both that a preacher should feel emotion himself and that his congregation should be allowed to share his feeling. The criterion of his sincerity must not be the excitement of the moment but the tenor of his ordinary life.

In contrast to the laymen, one's clerical colleagues probably prefer listening to a written sermon, not necessarily because that is the method to which they themselves are addicted, but because the manuscript is a guarantee that the preacher has paid them the compliment of taking trouble over his preparation. Also it shows his respect for the rapidity with which they will detect any mistakes of diction, grammar and syntax if he trusts to the inspiration of the moment. Such slips pass without comment in conversation, but in a formal allocution they stick out like a sore thumb.

From the speaker's point of view, the great advantage of preaching without a manuscript is that there is then no obstacle between him and his congregation: they can look each other straight in the eye. That is indeed an inestimable advantage to any speaker. If the audience know that he is looking at them, they are much more likely to look at him and pay attention to what he has to say. Anyone who has spoken much to gatherings of children will know how valuable and even necessary such a habit is. With adults, too, there should be a continuous traffic of visual communication. It is the best way of keeping the sermon alive and the congregation awake.

All this is tantamount to saying that, without a manuscript, it is easier for the personality of the preacher to get through. After all, is not that a fundamental part of his task; to make his own personality a vehicle for the conveyance of the divine message? The Christian follows a preacher who was identified with the 'Word', and we offer ourselves to be used as the voice of the same Word. Or, to put it another way, human personality may be the greatest of the sacraments, the fullest means by which God's revelation may be disclosed to succeeding generations, the outward and visible sign of the grace given to us for passing on to others. The least we can do is to try to remove whatever may hinder the full working of such a sacrament. If a script threatens to come between us and our people we must see whether we can dispense with it, and bring no disgrace upon our cause.

It is interesting to see how the television authorities on their own level grapple with this problem. They soon discovered that to show on their screen someone diligently reading a typescript was to invite boredom and consequent inattention. To dispense with a script altogether was out of the question, for the authorities themselves had to shoulder responsibility for what was said. The experiment was then tried of inducing the lecturer, for instance, to discard his manuscript and repeat its contents by rote. But this proved too difficult and nerve-racking for most speakers, and only a few of the foremost V.I.P.s were prepared to risk speaking at length without any note whatever. So was invented the clever idea of a gadget placed apparently behind the viewer's head and out of his sight. On this contraption rotated a tape from which the speaker or announcer read his words, and only the sophisticated could detect the artifice. It had, however, one defect: it made the reader cast his eyes to heaven, rather in the manner of 'The Soul's Awakening'. This disability was countered by providing him with a typescript to which he could occasionally cast down his eyes and so break the tension. Some of the professional announcers are so good at this game that it is hard to realise that they never look directly at you. So the process has come full circle from manuscript back to manuscript, though with a difference that cannot (so far) be imitated in the pulpit.

Against all this there are solid advantages to be enjoyed by the manuscript-reader. Most important is that he will probably be set free from all tendency to what, in other quarters, would be called stage fright. I say this although I remember at least one such reader who complained that he had spent a completely sleepless night before preaching at St. Paul's. And I remember Vernon Bartlett, who achieved such fame as a broadcaster, telling us that on the occasion of his first radio effort he could hardly get through his script because of his literally nauseating nervousness: in fact, he only held out just long enough to complete his piece before he rushed out of the building and was violently sick in the gutter.

Such nervousness, which is surely rare on the part of a reader, is common enough in the case of a speaker unsupported by either full manuscript or notes. In his case there is more excuse for it. He never knows when his mind is going to become a blank, and thoughts as well as words leave him stranded. Added to that is the humiliation of knowing that, whether he breaks down or not, his nervousness may become only too obvious to his hearers. But there he may pick up one crumb of comfort: his audience may well take his hesitation as a subtle compliment to themselves. At least he does not treat them with the bold effrontery of a pop singer or the condescension of a pedant. It never does to be too much at home in the pulpit.

Actually, if we practise our religion, there is no reason to be nervous at all. We are not entering upon some exercise or competition for our own honour; we are not showing off our own skill or expertise. We are God's messengers, fulfilling a commission from him. So long as we are doing what we believe he wants us to do, we can be completely calm and content, knowing that whatever happens to us will be overruled for the best.

Nevertheless, the manuscript-reader is perhaps happy in escaping so severe a trial of his faith. The reading of a written sermon can never, one would think, involve so severe a strain on the nerves as extempore preaching. The reader is also lucky in not having to worry overmuch about his verbal accuracy. He has settled all that in his study, where he has had sufficient leisure to select the words that best express his meaning. That must be at least part of the reason why politicians generally arm themselves with a manuscript. Even in the House, where they are not expected to read their speeches, they find it difficult to take their eyes off their notes. In their case it is more than the immediate audience they have to fear; there is the waiting Press and a public anxious for news, to say nothing of next morning's Hansard. The result of a clumsy word or an ill-turned phrase can be devastating. From all such accidents the reader is generally free.

He is also generally free from any sudden temptation to overmuch lightness or frivolity. The mere unfolding of his script on his entry into the pulpit tends to preserve the numinous atmosphere already engendered by the service. It is true that experienced orators can play upon the emotions of their congregation and sometimes achieve wonders by relaxing tension. By such means they may make the attention of their hearers a more flexible instrument for their own use. But the supreme reverence proper to worship is a very precious thing, and its loss should not lightly be risked.

For this reason among others those teachers were ill-advised who used to tell us that the preacher should model his style on that of barristers in the lawcourts. For one thing a modern lawcourt is an entirely different kind of structure from a church. A Gothic nave is one of the most difficult audience chambers in the world. A long hollow tunnel may increase noise, but it does not lend itself to clearness of enunciation. In this country we have made matters worse by placing the pulpit at one end of the nave, instead of in the middle. An even stronger contrast between church and lawcourt is provided by the atmosphere in which the speaking is done. I refer to the psychological atmosphere, which in the lawcourt is properly but surprisingly informal, whereas in the church (at least in the English church) it is by tradition extremely strict and rigid.

Many preachers have tried to mitigate the formality of the pulpit. Well-known examples from the last generation are Dick Sheppard and Studdert Kennedy. But even these experts could sometimes step over the line and destroy the very atmosphere they were seeking to build up. In our own time the incumbent of a well-known city parish, finding himself the happy possessor of two *ambones*, or pulpits, facing each other in his newly-restored church, put a preacher in each one and let them work out their theme in dialogue. His success in arousing the interest of the public varied in accordance with the prestige or 'image' of the speakers. In any case it is clear that in the use of such devices we are departing from the idea of the sermon as 'proclamation'. One does not wish to decry such experiments, which may indeed serve a very useful spearhead function, but there is a sense of relief in getting back to the idea of one man in the pulpit, surrounded by the numinous atmosphere of a truly religious service, doing his best to interpret to his people what he believes to be the will of God.

There is at least one other advantage that the reader enjoys over his colleague; he is able to judge more precisely the length of his discourse. It is true that the unscripted colleague can always glance at the watch on the pulpit ledge or on his wrist; but the worry is that he so often gets into a peroration from which he finds it difficult to extricate himself. The writer, by contrast, soon gets to know how many pages are needed to take up the allotted time and no more.

An important point for both to decide is how long that time should be. One realises how great have been the changes in this respect through the ages. We are aghast at the length of some of the Puritan sermons, and we find it hard to believe the story of the redoubtable preacher who, having talked steadily through the full period of his hour-glass, stood it on end and said, "Now we will go on to the second point." A generation ago we used to think a half-hour too long, but were prepared to settle for twenty minutes. Today the radio experts seem to prefer a quarter of an hour for what they consider a full-length sermon, while they are more likely to keep their early and late talks in the studio to five or perhaps ten minutes. They, of all men, should know how long the inexperienced public can keep its attention concentrated on the spoken word, even when the speaker is invisible. Normally it is much easier to pay attention when one can see the speaker, so that in church fifteen minutes may still be reckoned as a possible length, with twenty for special occasions when attention is already aroused and can be more easily maintained. Luckily the preacher who dispenses with a script can always keep his eye on the congregation and see when interest is beginning to flag.

Here again we are brought up against one of the disadvantages of a written sermon. If a preacher with a manuscript begins to sense that his congregation is becoming tired, it is not easy for him to leave out paragraphs or pages in the middle. To meet this difficulty it is generally recommended in books on public speaking that the practitioner should always have ready in his mind or on the paper a peroration which he can turn on at any moment in case of need. I have known Willie Temple on the platform do just that, and snatch victory out of what seemed certain defeat.

Coming now to the end of this somewhat involved and hesitating discussion of a most important subject, I offer the advice that the preacher should try to preach without a manuscript if he can. Only, he should be warned of the continual anxiety and stress that this method involves. However much he enjoys his work, he will never be without the weariness, the fever and the fret that are the constant companions of the extempore speaker. His consolation may be found in the fact that the more he endures the fever and the fret the less will be the weariness suffered by his people.

I imagine that your own experience as a teacher will prejudice you in favour of this view, but in case you feel that this judgment still tilts the scales too heavily against the reader, I can offer in compensation the following verdict on Ronnie Knox by Horton Davies (*Varieties of English Preaching*, p. 135):

> Knox, like the consummate stylist that he was, preached from a typewritten manuscript. He could do no other, with his sense of the exact word in the right order. Moreover, this practice safeguarded him from the possibilities of exaggeration and indiscretion, and from any fear that his fertile, darting mind might run away from him. He fully rehearsed his manuscript, which was marked with appropriate elocutionary signs, until he was almost word perfect.

To this is added a note from a contemporary:

> It is a unique gift of his to give by a sort of vocal legerdemain the impression, while reading, that he was still talking simply and directly to his hearers.

General Sermons

My dear Robert,

According to the sort of day on which they are preached, sermons may be divided into two classes, general and occasional. The general are those that are preached on any ordinary Sunday. I write 'ordinary' with some hesitation, because it is one of the glories of the church kalendar that each Sunday has its own particular character and is therefore like no other. Perhaps it would be better to stick to the ecclesiastical usage and say 'ferial', which distinguishes the ordinary Sundays from the days of special observance. In any case, I hope that it will be clear that in this section I am including only those sermons for which no particular circumstance indicates an obvious choice of topic for thought or theme for a discourse.

We must not suppose that a general sermon is less important than any other. If we are acting as God's ambassadors, it is his message that we have to deliver, and no one can say that it may be of no particular consequence on whatever day it is preached. We must expect results to follow from each sermon we deliver. It is true that we are not likely ourselves always to know what those results are (although congregations are not unready with their comments), but years afterwards we may be surprised to hear, if not of actual 'conversions', yet of changed lives and accepted vocations as a consequence of the words we have been privileged to utter. We cast our bread upon the waters and may never know whose need it satisfies.

At least we know that the needs are many and that we must

try to satisfy them all. Every sermon must have its element of proclamation and challenge, but not every sermon must be directed to the unconverted. The committed churchmen have their needs, too. They have to be trained in the knowledge and practice of their faith, and this becomes more and more important in proportion as their education becomes secularised and they enjoy less specifically Christian teaching in their youth. In other words, there is the whole sphere of edification to be considered, the building up of the believer in the art of Christian living. Knowledge of this art can by no means be taken for granted, and under modern conditions the onus of communicating it to the general public must rest more and more upon the preacher. The need for his skilled services increases day by day.

It is, as always, clear that if we are to perform this task efficiently, we must attract and hold the attention of our hearers. To this end one of the greatest hindrances is monotony, and one of the greatest helps — variety. Here we have the invaluable assistance of the changing seasons of the Church's year; in the first half, from Advent to Whit Sunday, we follow the life of Christ with its appropriate doctrines, and in the second, through Trinity to Advent, we consider the moral implications of our Christian profession. But more important still, from the point of view of cultivating variety, every single Sunday has its own special flavour conveyed by its own 'proper', its special lections and prayers.

Such a variety of subject is a God-given asset to the preacher: it should of itself do much to overcome the monotony of our own personality and style. Yet it is remarkable how many preachers are ready to dispense with it in whole or in part. I once knew a cathedral dean, formerly a notable London orator, who actually boasted that never once in the whole course of his ministry had he ever preached from the collect, epistle, gospel, or lessons for the day. I suppose there is something of the rebel in all of us, but to carry independence that far seems both to make things unduly difficult for oneself and also to deprive one's congregation of a valuable means of identifying their own devotions with those of the world-wide Church, the worshipping people of God.

A further advantage of a close adherence to the kalendar is that it gives us an all-round knowledge of the Christian faith. If left to themselves, most clergymen are inclined to expatiate on those doctrines that particularly appeal to themselves. A variant of the same tendency is often to be noticed if they are fervent adherents of some special school or party. In that case, the bulk of their sermons will centre upon those doctrines that are specially characteristic of the group to which they belong. However valuable or vital those doctrines may be, it is obvious that, even when put together, their sum total is still something less than the whole complex of Christian doctrine, and that by so much must the grasp of the congregation upon the totality of the faith be weakened. This failure to present to one's people the complete faith must arouse serious misgiving in the mind of anyone who believes in the reality of revelation. Ought they not to receive the *whole* doctrine of God? Against any such unwitting dereliction of duty on the part of a preacher, adherence to the kalendar is a strong protection.

Another powerful protection against both monotony and partiality is to be found in the habit of preaching courses of sermons. I shall consider later some of the special circumstances in which this device can be employed, but in the meantime we can notice how valuable it is for both priest and people. For the former it demands a much more sustained effort in preparation than does the single, isolated sermon. It also compels him to take a bird's-eye view of whole tracts of Christian teaching and so to estimate the relative importance of the individual parts. For the congregation it involves a sustained effort of interest beyond what is required for the single sermon; but because of the quickened attention aroused by the continuity of the course, the effort may be more spontaneous, and consequently less

burdensome, than is normally the case. We have only to remember how those powerful representatives of mass media,
television and radio, employ the device of even quite long series
and courses in nearly all their departments, to realise that we
should be forfeiting a decided advantage if we did not use the
method to the limit of our capacity for the propagation of the
gospel.

Most of us are well accustomed to the practice of arranging
special courses of sermons in Advent and Lent, and we are
aware how valuable they are in bringing out the meaning of
those particular seasons. There is no reason why the method
should not be associated with some element in the general life
and teaching of the Church, apart from any particular season.
Such a method would be specially valuable for any man who
has to preach in the same pulpit twice every Sunday. Why
should he not devote one of his sermons to the devotional teaching of the day and the other to some continuous course of
regular instruction? He might have to do some extra reading for
this, and spend some extra time on preparation, but I feel sure
that both he and his flock would enjoy the result. It might even
increase the size of his congregation.

You may notice next how important it is in preaching
'general' sermons to emphasise the truly great themes of the
gospel. It is always easy, if one sticks solely to the lectionary, to
become absorbed in biblical stories and incidents: the effort to
translate them into the terms of modern life is so utterly
fascinating. No wonder if our congregations begin to share our
enthusiasm, and become so absorbed in the details that before
long they cannot see the wood for the trees. To counter this
tendency we must from time to time see to it that the fundamental issues do not escape us.

In doing so we should take care to remind our people of the
turning-points of human life and destiny. We must not allow
ourselves to be put off by the feeling that, just because these
issues are universal and fundamental, the congregation will

have thought much about them already. Actually people think very little about the common things, which in any case always appear fresh when seen through a fresh pair of eyes. We must ourselves have pondered over them long and deeply because of the necessary circumstances of our profession. It would seem to be our bounden duty to give the congregation the benefit of our thoughts. After all, we are fellow travellers on the same road and we are glad to have each other's helpful comments on the journey. And the parson is not only a fellow traveller: he is an official guide.

Instances of great themes abound and are well worth consideration. Take the most fundamental of all, the meaning of God. The world-wide fame accorded to Bishop John Robinson's paperback *Honest to God* revealed without gainsaying how hungry men are for some reliable news of the unseen. The truth of the immanence of God which the bishop emphasised so strongly in that book was and is valid enough, but it is only half the truth. Why not take care that your own hearers do not miss the other half? It should not be too difficult to line in for them the pictures Jesus drew of a loving, heavenly father who is more richly personal than any human person can ever be. If one has tried a prentice hand at that, why not go on to tackle the person of Christ and try to explain what is meant by an incarnation, a subject about which the most childish mistakes are constantly made? Or for the matter of that why not take Christianity itself? What is it: a creed, an institution, a code of morals, a culture, an attitude to life, or, as St. Paul and St. John so obviously believed, just plain incorporation into Christ?

If such themes seem too much in the air for the average congregation, it should be easy to come down to earth with a practical explanation of some one or other of the main Christian virtues. Faith, hope and love are obvious candidates for inclusion—the favourite, as always, being love. There probably never was a time when this virtue was so much talked about and so little understood. From the pop festival to the professor's class-room, in song and lecture, the word is discussed in a multitude of meanings, and only the comparatively few get back to the gospel teaching of 'universal and unselfish service of others'. It is not only the adolescents who need guidance here.

It would not be surprising if in our generation hope took the place of love as the centre of interest. After all, we have recently made great strides in the matter of mutual service. Our hospitals, pensions and health services, organised as they are on a national scale, are far more efficient than the old casual charity could ever be. On the other hand, where hope is concerned we are probably worse off than we have been for many generations. It is not merely that the prevalence of strikes and the manufacture of nuclear weapons have brought near the possibility of mutual destruction, but we have to a large extent lost our vision of what is to happen to us when the mutual destruction is over. We have achieved a new interest in what the theologians call 'eschatology' only to discover that, as far as science goes, there may be no room for an eschatology at all. As faith has become weaker, hope has disappeared. But to have something to look forward to is both the greatest of present pleasures and the strongest incentive to active preparation for the future. The man who helps the world to recover its hope is rendering the greatest possible service to mankind.

As for faith, the third of these virtues, what we need to emphasise is the importance of an affirmative attitude towards life. The present determination on the part of many young people not to become involved but to 'do their own thing' is a sign of a lack of faith not only in their fellows and in contemporary society but also in the whole constitution and purpose of the universe. This negative attitude spells ruin both for the individuals who succumb to it and for any society in which it spreads. It is the duty of the Christian preacher, above all men, to dispel this miasma, to build up faith in the good purposes of God, and in his power to accomplish them. It is only as we have a positive belief in the goodness of God and of his universe (in spite of all appearances to the contrary) that we are likely to maintain our courage and our determination to play a worthy part in everyday life.

Beside such a series of great themes we can easily set a list of great words, which will serve our purpose equally well. It is interesting how a single word can enshrine vast treasures of Christian teaching. It is equally interesting to notice how habitually it can be used by Christian people without any real penetration into the depths of its meaning. Long association and frequent liturgical use can give a certain numinous quality to well-known words of which even the regular church-goer might find it difficult to analyse the connotation. Take for instance some of the words most frequently on our lips in church, such as righteousness, salvation, glory, and ask yourself what they mean to you. Unless you are used to the exercise, it will probably take some time to find a good answer, and you will realise how grateful will be the average congregation for a little help in this direction.

Unless one has access to bigger works, Alan Richardson's *Theological Word Book of the Bible* will be found a useful guide in this connection. It will there be seen that God himself is *righteousness* and is therefore the norm of righteousness (i.e. the quality of being right) in others. Even in the Old Testament, this trait included vindication of the helpless and showing mercy to the poor. In the New Testament it is expanded to embrace those finer qualities that are generally associated with Christian agape as well as with the classical notion of justice or fairness. And, all through, this complex of virtues is combined with that spiritual quality which arouses them, maintains them in being, and leads to the ultimate perfection which is salvation, in other words 'the grace of God'.

Such a consideration makes it easy for us to realise that *salvation* itself is much more of an omnibus word than those who use it so lightly and frequently have time to remember. It implies a certain wholeness of well-being, both of soul and body, which should make it a favoured term in days when psychosomatic healing has become a common topic. It suggests that type of perfection for which the kingdom of God is the proper environment. That does not mean that we must wait for heaven for its beginning. It was actually introduced to mankind in the life and teaching of Jesus himself; his parables and miracles displayed the nature of the messianic reign which was the epitome of salvation. To enter within that reign is the experience of every believer when he becomes a conscious member of Christ. But all this is only the dawning of salvation. "The path of the righteous is as the light of dawn that shineth more and more unto the perfect day." No doubt, both for the individual and for the universe, there will be many clouds across the sky before the millennium is reached, but we can enjoy the healthful sunshine now, and wait in confidence within the sphere of salvation for the promised end to be disclosed.

Glory is the word that describes better than any other the condition of the end. But it is a term that has almost dropped out of our language except for liturgical use. We still coin adjectives and adverbs from it—you can still wear a 'glorious' dress at 'glorious' Goodwood, and a man can still get 'gloriously' drunk on his winnings, but both neglect and misuse show how far we have departed from the spirit of the New Testament. All the more reason for us to try to restore some of its former splendour.

In the Old Testament, glory seems, oddly enough, to derive from the notion of *weight*, and may be associated with the specially heavy robes worn on ceremonial occasions by high-ranking officials. In this connection it has been compared with our phrase 'a man of substance'. In the New Testament it has acquired much of the Greek regard for reputation, so that the idea of 'fame' seems almost to supersede that of official importance. But the New Testament adds its own special emphasis to the word in its association of 'glory' with 'light'. It was this kind of glory that appeared at Jesus's birth, that revealed him as

E

Messiah in his transfiguration, and would accompany his appearance at his Second Coming.

So the biblical notion of glory, like that of salvation, is a complex one, and has some relation to the physical as well as to the spiritual side of our nature. It describes, in any case, the proper atmosphere in which the Christian man should live and to which in its perfection he should aspire when he dies. To be assured of it as a present possession should give courage to the congregation, and help to keep them in that confident frame of mind which should be characteristic of all Christian people.

That is all we need to say for the moment about 'general' sermons. I hope it is enough to start a young preacher thinking how best to expand the list. It would be a good thing for you to accumulate some of your best sermons on these and suchlike subjects. You can go over them and improve them at your leisure. You will then always have a reserve to fall back upon in case of emergency, and you will be helped to clear your own mind on some of the outstanding points of faith. Bishop Gore was not ashamed to say that he wrote his classic *Body of Christ* for just that purpose, 'to clear his own mind'. In a day of considerable doubt and confusion we may well enhance our value as preachers by following his example, and by making sure we know what gospel we have to preach. The thinking out of great themes for 'general' sermons should certainly help us to be clear about our own faith.

LETTER 9

Occasional Sermons

My dear Robert,
We come now to the consideration of the special or 'occasional' sermon. The term is much more commonly used overseas than in England, and is intended to distinguish the spasmodic from the routine. We get a hint of that meaning in liturgical use when the 'occasional' offices are contrasted with the 'daily' office. If it is used of sermons, its effect is to distinguish between orations delivered on special occasions and those delivered in the everyday course of the Church's life. The term may even be transferred from the sermon to the preacher, so that you may read a notice in the newspaper to the effect that "the occasional preacher was the Reverend Mr. So-and-so". Here we may take the phrase 'occasional sermon' as applying to a discourse delivered on some special day, or by a visiting preacher, or in the course of some service other than the daily office or regular eucharist.

First, then, for the discourse delivered on some special day. This may be a local celebration such as a patronal festival (commemoration of the patron saint) or an occasion of national or even universal concern. In any case it is a tremendous opportunity for the preacher. Everyone is agog with expectation, especially the children, and everyone is ready to listen, at least at the outset. It is important that the preacher should not throw away this extra awareness: he must strike while the iron is hot. If he begins by talking about something that has no obvious relation to the subject in hand, he may exercise the art

67

of suspense for a few moments, but not for long; and once attention has been lost it will be difficult to recapture. It is much better for him to start with the subject of the precise occasion, and to mention the reason for the celebration in his opening sentences.

At the same time he must not allow himself or his audience to become so engrossed in the temporal context of the occasion that they are left thinking, in the end, that this was the main or only subject of the discourse. If, for instance, the occasion is the dedication of a new building, some reference to the design and suitability of the structure will be thoroughly appropriate, but the spiritual opportunity will be lost if the discourse resolves itself into a lecture on architecture. Travelling through the allied lines during the First World War, I attended a church parade at which a very vigorous harangue was delivered by a young chaplain. His theme was the current struggle, and as far as I could judge his main point was that the enemy soldiers were devils. It turned out to be his only point and I was not surprised that his own soldiers, who formed the congregation, became decidedly restless. They had not come to hear a discourse on the character of the enemy, and in any case they knew more about that than the preacher did. As always, so especially in an occasional sermon, one must remember that the purpose of all preaching is the proclamation of Christ. If we have not used the golden opportunity offered by increased awareness to present that plea, then we have failed indeed.

An extra measure of the awareness aroused by the occasional sermon is enjoyed by a visiting preacher. Even if he is only filling a temporary vacancy and comes to preach in the ordinary round of the parochial services, he still has the advantage of novelty. His is a new voice and a new figure in the pulpit; people will be interested in him, his appearance, his manner, his gestures. Everybody will be expecting something fresh, not new necessarily, but fresh in its liveliness and power to hold. If he is associated with some special department of the Church's work — charity, education, missions — he will be expected to say something about it, whether he is pleading specifically for it or not. If he is not, then he should deal with it only lightly, and not use the occasion as an opportunity for beating his own drum. But in either case, on a subject with which he is so familiar, he ought to be able to say something interesting to people for whom it is comparatively unknown territory. Above all, he must remember that at the back of his own speciality lies the age-long message which it is the business of every preacher to proclaim. He will then enjoy the privilege of trying to make 'the old familiar truth shine with a new uncommon lustre', a privilege that comes more naturally to a stranger than to a parish priest who has been doing the same thing in his own way twice a Sunday for many years.

Anyone who, even without representing any specialised interest, finds himself frequently functioning as an 'occasional' preacher will be well advised to pay particular attention to the preparation of two or three sermons on fundamental issues of the Christian faith, with a view to preaching them over and over again in different churches. There is nothing reprehensible in such repetition. If a sermon is worth preaching once, it is worth preaching many times, so long as the audience is not already familiar with it.

A saintly and hard-working archdeacon, who in the course of his duties had to visit many churches, could never bring himself to preach any sermon more than once. He felt that no sermon was ever quite so real to him as on its first delivery. The result was that his sermons never acquired that extra polish and apt-ness of phrase that would have driven home his message, and he had to suffer the mortification of hearing his own clergy dis-close his error. Actually the sermon should become not less but more real the oftener you preach it. You yourself know what it sounds like; you have got your paragraphs in logical order: you have got the best words you are capable of choosing to express your meaning; you can give your whole attention to the delivery of your message and to judging its effect by the faces of your congregation. How otherwise could such mission preachers as Wesley and Whitefield, Studdert Kennedy and Billy Graham have spoken with such assurance and effect to the crowds who thronged to hear them?

The greatest sermon I ever heard was preached by Martin Luther King at St. Paul's. He had, of course, that glorious voice (a Paul Robeson in the pulpit) which echoed like an organ diapason round the vast building and tore at your heartstrings even before you had time to give attention to what he had to say. I had no doubt that he had preached the sermon many times before, so that he never had to hesitate for a word. He was also a professor of English literature so that his diction and his illustrative material were perfect. These technicalities having been adjusted before ever he came into the pulpit, the personality of the preacher was set free to convey as an ambassador God's message to his people. He spoke little of the disabilities under which he believed his folk to be suffering: his utter sincerity and his intense emotion were those of 'a dying man speaking to dying men' and holding out to all the opportunity of a new and glorious life. When we returned to the vestry I felt constrained to tell him that, old man that I was, I thanked God that I had lived long enough to hear that sermon.

If anyone has lingering doubts about the advisability of repeating sermons, he might ponder for a moment this thought. One of the questions now debated among New Testament scholars is whether Jesus was mainly prophet or teacher, and whether we are to think of him as a reformer haranguing the multitude with some unique and earth-shaking message, or as a rabbi sitting among his disciples, repeating over and over again stories and lessons for them to learn by heart. I have no doubt, personally, that both elements entered into Jesus's preaching, and I can see no reason why we should not follow his example in the second instance as well as in the first. No doubt your own experience as a teacher will lend support to this view.

Giving some attention now to the special times and occasions on which a visiting preacher may be expected to function, we cannot avoid the conclusion that the most popular is the harvest festival, a feast that is of comparatively recent introduction. In spite of its lack of historical tradition, it has made for itself a place in the affections of English people hardly surpassed by the Feast of the Assumption among Roman Catholics. At least that is true of country churches, whatever may be said of the towns, though even there it probably brings in more 'fringe' worshippers than any more strictly ecclesiastical occasion. There is no need for us to feel superior towards it: we can hardly go wrong in giving special attention to this spontaneous expression of popular religion. Probably nothing would have appealed more strongly to the heart of Francis of Assisi, if he had been lucky enough to think of it. No doubt it is a semi-pagan occasion, but is it any the worse for that? Certainly the historic Church had no hesitation about baptizing heathen customs into Christ. It is possible that such hybrids appeal to something deep down in our nature that outdates all historical religion. Within the traditional sphere of revelation we may remember that the Old Testament Jews had three main festivals each year, and they were all harvest festivals.

Both seed-time and harvest give golden opportunities of drawing spiritual lessons from nature, as Jesus and Paul knew very well. But the preacher, unless he is a countryman, should beware of being too technical. That, however, is a danger that dogs the footsteps of every seeker for the apt illustration. Once, preaching on Tyneside, I felt rather pleased with a long illustration I had drawn from an engineering process, only to be considerably deflated afterwards in the vestry when the church-wardens (from the Armstrong Whitworth works) burst out in chorus, "You forgot the mould." My only consolation was that at least they had been listening.

A more mundane, but none the less serious, danger for the harvest preacher is that of physical contact with the decorations. If he is wearing his best stole, the row of tomatoes on the pulpit ledge can be quite devastating. And his best point can be ruined if he knocks a small pot-plant from the same point of vantage into the lap of the colonel's lady underneath.

Leaving the harvest festival on one side, it should be remembered that the occasional offices, properly so-called, touch a whole range of emotions and provide excellent opportunities of applying Christian teaching to the crises of human life. I am not, by exception, very much in favour of sermons at funerals. I can quite understand a warm-hearted pastor wishing to take public leave of a loved parishioner and to use his or her life as a pointer to Christ, but generally the emotions of the principal mourners are at too great a tension to make this an appropriate moment for oratory. One can quite understand, too, that the funeral of some considerable personage may demand a public effort to estimate his life and achievement, although that is now generally done later at a memorial service. But when the panegyric (as some of our friends unashamedly call it) is demanded for all and sundry, the result tends to become formal or boring or even slightly comic. On the whole it seems wisest to omit the sermon altogether or to ensure that it is delivered by someone who knew the deceased well and can be trusted to speak with both sincerity and dignity.

An occasional sermon that falls to the lot of bishops is the address at a Confirmation. This is indeed one of the happiest occasions in a bishop's ministry. Here he has the chance of speaking to young people at the most impressionable point of their development. Here, if anywhere, he must practise the art of his craft. He must not talk down to the candidates or speak above their heads. He must not tire them by being too long, or belittle the occasion by being too short. He must be simple and direct without overloading the sentiment or bullying the candidates. His object is not to frighten them but to strengthen them. He cannot discuss with them the whole of Christian doctrine, but he can at least try to reinforce what the parish priest has already taught them in their preparation classes.

Most bishops take so many confirmations that they have to be constantly on the watch lest the whole proceeding, including the sermon, become mechanised or formal. The difficulty is that one must always emphasise the same essential truths, and each time one feels that this is the only occasion on which these young people will have this conspectus put before them with the corollary that they are pledging themselves here and now to act upon it. Personally, I always felt that the three points to be emphasised were confession of Christ, the gift of the Holy Spirit, and admission to Holy Communion. (I am not at all sure what the priorities should be now in cases where the Holy Spirit is held to be fully given in baptism and where Holy Communion is habitually received long before confirmation.) I used to find relief from the monotony of constant repetition by fitting these points into the especial framework provided by the changes in the ecclesiastical kalendar. The nearest Sunday, red-letter day, or even black-letter day would not only provide apt illustrations but would also help to fix the date in the congregation's minds so that they could the more easily remember the anniversary. I hope it also helped some of the young people to realise how long and honourable was the line of saints they had solemnly elected to join. (You will not fail to notice that in dealing with a bishop's address I am anticipating a long career for you in the ministry!)

If the address at a confirmation is a voluntary offering on the part of the bishop, at a wedding there is no escape. An address must be given either in the form of a fixed homily or an extempore talk or a prescribed passage of scripture. Such an address is not intended solely for bride and groom, though it is often directed to them particularly. The priest is intended to use it as an opportunity of instructing the general congregation as well as such members of the unthinking multitude as find themselves present. The neglect or misuse of this opportunity is largely responsible for the quite appalling ignorance of the meaning of marriage in England today. It is not enough, there-fore, for the preacher to devote his discourse to a pretty but sentimental eulogy of married love, about which his audience probably know as much as he does. What they do not know, and what it is his business to teach them, is what constitutes a valid marriage and what are the principles upon which the rules regulating it are laid down. This is surely an opportunity not to be missed. The celebrant acts here as agent of both Church and State, and on this point (apart from some difference over the question of divorce) the two are in essential agreement. For both alike the essentials of a valid marriage are threefold: absence of diriment impediment, unforced mutual consent, and publicity. These are complementary to, but must be clearly distinguished from, the three 'causes for which matrimony was ordained', as set forth in the Book of Common Prayer. It would make a considerable difference to the common attitude towards marriage if they were generally understood. It might even make some difference to the sightseers who flock to a fashionable wedding, if they were told, under the head of 'publicity', that they themselves perform a part in the ceremony as witnesses on behalf of both Church and State. They might even be dis-suaded from clambering on the seats and persuaded, instead, to pray, really and truly pray, for the blessing of God on the couple now being joined together to form a new social unit in a Christian society.

Here again, as at a confirmation, a practical detail is im-portant. Do not let the sermon be too long. It is said that once, in the days when a marriage to be legal must be celebrated before three p.m., Ronald Knox, striving to do what was expected of him as a famous preacher, was in full spate as the mystic hour approached. He was blind to all signals, and after anxious consultation behind the scenes a verger was sent to draw him out of the pulpit so that the necessary parts of the ceremony could be performed before the clock struck. Another practical detail: if a full sermon is to be preached, it is a real kindness to provide a couple of chairs on which the bride and groom may sit during the discourse.

Another occasion on which a short sermon is indicated is an ordination. Here by common consent the bishop is relieved of the obligation to preach and the duty is conferred, as a mark of honour on some visiting preacher. Often it devolves on some young don, who, having little knowledge (so far) of clerical life, but full of enthusiasm for his own studies, uses the occasion to disentangle some abstruse point of doctrine or settle some outstanding ecclesiastical dispute. Actually, the proper subject of the sermon is already laid down in the first rubric to the ordinal. It is "to declare the duty and office of such as come to be ordained, to show how necessary that order is in the Church of Christ, and to explain how the people ought to esteem those upon whom hands have been laid". This analysis covers a pretty wide field: it is generally found necessary to choose only one point out of it if the preacher is to keep within the limits regarded as reasonable for an already long service.

In any case it is well for the preacher to remember that on this occasion it is not his sermon but the service itself which is the really important thing. His purpose should be to make the 'ordering' come alive for all who are taking part in it—and that includes the laity whose prayers form a valuable, if not actually essential, part of the service. A request for those prayers, as well as a word of encouragement and hope for the ordinands, will be an appropriate element in the discourse.

Perhaps to this rapid review of 'occasional' sermons one word may be added about preaching on board ship. A clerical passenger may well feel shy about offering his services, but a ship is generally a very friendly place and a word with the purser (once things have settled down and he has a moment to spare) will soon make clear what the situation is. Many captains like to take their own service, but some are glad to accept the help of an occasional preacher. If the service is held in the lounge this will be found a very comfortable place in which to preach, provided the weather is right. But if for some reason one has to preach on the hurricane deck, this will be found the worst auditorium in the world. Usually ships' services are much better attended than those on shore, but on such an occasion it requires a superlative kind of elocution to reach the deaf man on the back row. I did once hear a missionary speak to a crowded congregation on deck for a whole hour: when he stopped, the audience, which by this time included a large proportion of the ship's crew, demanded more. The speaker craved a moment's respite while he went below to get a drink, and then came back and kept us enthralled for another half-hour. But such eloquence and grace are not granted to many of us.

This rather heartening story must conclude my description of general and occasional sermons. I hope it will serve to fortify your recognition of the variety of interest at the disposal of a preacher. In my next letter I shall get down to the practical task of the preacher in his choice of subject and actual preparation of a sermon.

Choice of Subject

My dear Robert,

It is terribly important that anyone seeking ordination should from the outset make up his mind how he is going to approach his duty as a preacher. Is he to be content with the status of the gifted amateur, or is he to aim at becoming a real professional? Happily, even without conscious decision, many of the clergy achieve the latter condition through sheer constant practice. Evidence for such a judgment can be heard in the sigh of relief that escapes the audience when at a public meeting a parson gets up to speak after several semi-articulate laymen have tried and failed. Perhaps one ought not to mention it, but a few years ago the Mansion House officials gave it as their opinion that the speeches at the Bishops' Dinner were the best of the year, and the Toastmasters' Company officially adjudged the then Archbishop of Canterbury to be the best after-dinner speaker of the period.

Fortunately or unfortunately, there are so many aspects to the parson's life and he has so many varied duties to perform that it is very easy for him to become a 'jack of all trades and master of none'. But an easy acquiescence in an amateur status is still a calamity. Ours is an age of specialists, as everyone knows, for instance, from the example of the medical and engineering professions. Everyone knows, too, how the professional artist looks down upon the mere amateur. Today even the army does its recruiting under the slogan, "Join the Professionals".

Preaching is the part of his work that brings the parson most clearly before the public. It is important, therefore, that he should take as much trouble over acquiring the special expertise of this task as, shall we say, an accountant or personnel manager is expected to do over his. For a time at least he should be willing to bend all his studies this way, and throughout his career he should try to improve his knowledge and to keep in touch with changing techniques.

Apprenticeship to the office of a preacher does not stop short at the acquisition of technical skills, such as voice production, literary craftsmanship and theological scholarship. It applies also to the whole content of experience gained in everyday life within the human environment, to say nothing of specifically religious training and discipline. It is the whole man who preaches, and it is his whole life that gives point to his sermon: he preaches through his character.

It was an express purpose of these letters to discuss preaching as an art. We have now been impelled to qualify this intention by pointing out that preaching is much more than an art: it is a life. Nevertheless, it is precisely through this art of preaching that the preacher's life finds specific expression. He must learn not to give, through carelessness or incompetence, a wrong impression of that teaching for which he stands and by which presumably his own life is directed. If he does, he dishonours himself, the Church and his Master. No further assurance need be given of the need for thorough preparation.

When we descend from the general to the particular, and begin to think of the preparation of an individual sermon, we are faced at once with the prime necessity of understanding exactly what the occasion is. If we are to hit the mark, we must at least see the target clearly. It is said to have been the custom of Winnington-Ingram, the lovable Bishop of London, to prepare a fresh sermon each week, which he preached first on the Sunday and then repeated as often as he was called upon to preach on the following weekdays. On one Sunday he had preached a timely and eloquent sermon about safety on the roads. The next day he was preaching at the clothing of a nun. In full flight he sensed that his remarks were hardly appropriate and tried to cover his lapse. "You see, my dear Sisters, that I have chosen a rather unusual subject for my address today. But it is very advisable for you, in the midst of your sheltered lives, to know what dangers you may meet when you venture from your convent to the roads outside."

If we are to avoid the necessity for that kind of apology, we must envisage as clearly as possible both the audience we are to address and the occasion that calls them together. If we can satisfy ourselves on those points we shall find that half our agitation is removed at the outset. Even royalty requires this reassurance. When King George VI attended his memorable thanksgiving service at St. Paul's, he was expected at its conclusion to address the waiting crowd. He was led in procession down the nave to the great west doors, but there he stopped and refused to have them opened until he knew exactly what was going to happen. When he was told that, as soon as the two porters had opened the doors, he would find a microphone on the top step and that he would advance to it and read his address to the people who filled the whole space in the forecourt and down Ludgate Hill, he was perfectly happy, and the proceedings were completed without a hitch. Everyone who has had to face a great concourse without being able first to visualise its setting will understand and appreciate the reason for the royal hesitation.

The preacher will want to know about his congregation, whether it is juvenile or adult or mixed, and about the occasion: whether the sermon is meant to be the climax of the service, or to lead up to something else, or indeed, apart from a few prayers, to be the only thing. This may all seem very obvious; but it is exceedingly important, as it affects both the type and length of discourse. Organisers of programmes have an odd way of expecting a visiting preacher to know such things by instinct.

I once preached to a lecture society under the impression that I had been invited to give one of the lectures, only to find, when I had held the fort for an hour or so, that all I had been expected to do was to say a few devotional sentences by way of winding up the term's session.

Charles Smyth, in his learned and interesting book *The Art of Preaching*, seeks to reassure us by saying that any man can preach who reads his Bible, says his prayers, and loves his people. But he is also very decided about the meticulous care that the preacher must devote to his task. He must above all speak to his hearers' condition; and to do that he must know in general who they are and in what devotional mood they are likely to be when he addresses them.

Then and only then is he in a position to decide what type of sermon he will preach. Will it be a run-of-the-mill sermon with something in it for everyone, helping them to face the normal difficulties of everyday life; or will it be a direct challenge to the careless, calling them in the name of Christ to commit themselves definitely to his cause; or will it be an exposition of some biblical passage taken from the lections for the day? We have already in an earlier letter divided sermons into the three main categories of proclamation, teaching and devotion. We may find it useful at this stage to examine some sub-divisions of these types a little more closely.

Probably the most common, if not the most popular kind of sermon in the Anglican communion today, although it is not widely known by this name, is the Prone. In medieval times the prone was the part of the liturgy most closely connected with the sermon at High Mass. Presently the term came to be narrowed down to the sermon itself. The Eucharist is still the one regular service at which the Prayer Book orders a sermon. Now that that particular service has returned to something like its earlier popularity, the sermon preached at it has acquired particular importance.

It is inevitable and proper that a sermon at this point should be subordinate to the liturgy itself. Coming, as it does, after the scripture readings, it will prepare the hearts and minds of the congregation for the consecration and communion that are to follow. No doubt it will look beyond this immediate purpose to the environment in life as a whole, but, even if it does so, the guidelines will be set by the service. It follows that the discourse, taking its colour from the liturgy, should be based on some element in the 'proper' for the day, generally the collect, epistle or gospel, or the Old Testament reading, if there is one.

Some preachers may find this convention too cramping for their own taste, but it is still a good thing to learn and to observe it. It prevents one from roaming at large and so dissociating oneself and one's congregation from the service in hand. It should be the aim of the preacher to enlist the intelligent co-operation of his people in making to the best of their ability a combined, complete, coherent act of worship to almighty God. If the service and the sermon are not in tune with each other, there will be left some untoward feeling of inadequacy and failure.

This general rule of liturgical coherence should still be in our mind when we come to consider another type of sermon, the Expository. Preaching, as we know, is the proclamation of the word of God: the expository sermon both proclaims and explains that word. It should be obvious that much point will be given to the exposition if it is devoted, not to some passage of scripture that has nothing to do with the service in hand, but to some extract from the lessons actually read in the course of the service. It is true that this method may limit the preacher in the choice of a text, but it should give valuable help in the choice of his subject. And that is a great time-saver.

No type of preaching is easy, but the expository sermon should be less difficult than most. The main reason is precisely that the preacher is here given more help than elsewhere. He is not left cudgelling his brains in search of a subject; that is given him in the chosen passage. So also is the outline of his sermon.

His first task is to explain his text in relation to its context—not just the meaning of the individual words but the idea conveyed by the passage as a whole, even if in doing so he has to give a brief account of the entire book from which it is taken. Following upon this introduction he will draw out in succession two or three points suggested by his reflections on the text so far. In doing so he will take care to keep his divisions as clear and simple as possible. For this purpose the example of most previous preaching may well be ignored. Earlier preachers had much more time at their disposal than we have. Today there is infinitely more competition for the people's leisure. If we hope to compete on favourable terms, we must 'keep it short' and simple. But in no case must we finish our point without showing its relevance to everyday faith and practice. The congregation must not be left wondering 'what it was all about'.

Discussion of the expository sermon leads naturally to the thought of that related type which we may call the Instructional sermon. As we have already seen, the distinction between preaching and teaching has never been entirely clear, in spite of the excellent work done by theologians in trying to differentiate between *kerygma* and *didache* in the New Testament. The two fail to fit neatly into separate compartments. There must be some element of teaching in every challenge to serve Christ: conversely if there is no challenge in a piece of teaching, it has missed its mark.

Why not then make a virtue of necessity and, at least on some occasions, preach sermons that are candidly intended to teach? Most of us already have samples at hand in our confirmation classes. For some at least of the parochial clergy they represent the happiest hours of their ministry. The talks they have given so often have become by now quite smooth and polished, with all the outlines carefully planned and all the happiest illustrations in the right places. After a few years of ministry they probably represent the best we are capable of doing in this direction. Why not give the evening congregation the benefit of them? If one is afraid that adults may be offended at being treated as children, one can always try the oblique approach: "You know that I have just begun this year's confirmation classes: I think you may like to hear what I am teaching your children." Many people learn best when they are 'listening in' to the instruction being given to others. This method may also have the added advantage of removing from the parents' minds any possible suspicion of what you actually are teaching their children. And in any case it does us all good to hear from time to time a fairly rapid summary of Christian faith and practice.

Having broken the ice in this way, we might very well go on to suggest other lecture-sermons on other Sunday evenings. Such a venture should surely be a relief to an incumbent who has to preach twice each Sunday to the same congregation, provided, of course, that he can find, or make, time to prepare such talks adequately. I can never see why, if the parson 'prones' in the morning, he should not frankly lecture in the evening. The broadcasting people set us a good example when they began inviting members of various professions and practitioners of various skills to come to the microphone and give introductory talks for fifteen or twenty minutes on their particular expertise.

I have always thought that these popular lectures set a good example for our sermons. We could hardly do better than occasionally attempt to rival their standard and tell people what, for instance, our own subject, theology, is all about. After all, we have been trained for just this kind of effort. And if the mere thought of it makes us tear our hair over those books we sold and those notebooks we burnt when we left the theological college, it serves us right. What other craftsman ever dreams of getting rid of his tools as soon as he has qualified?

If we have been sensible and kept in touch with our academic studies during the course of our ministry, we shall surely enjoy the opportunity of introducing our people to the most fascinating of all subjects. We can begin by asking what is theology, what is its relation to religion, what is the difference between natural and revealed theology, and what are its different branches. Before long the congregation will be showing a desire to know something from the scientific point of view about church history and doctrine, about the structure of the Old and New Testaments, about liturgiology and ethics, enough to keep them going for the whole of our ministry among them. We have long complained about the yawning(!) gulf between the pew and the pulpit; well, here is our chance to bridge it. No longer must we let it be said that the language in which theologians speak to one another is an unknown tongue to the men in the pews.

To one objection we must pay considerable respect. There will certainly be some who will say that they do not like this type of sermon because it is not 'practical'. At all costs we must not let this objection become valid. We should never end such a lecture-sermon without asking what effect the specific piece of theology about which we have been preaching should have on our attitude to life and the world. That will be a salutary exercise for speakers and listeners alike. Without such a proviso it is possible for our choicest pieces of biblical and historical theology to become as desiccated as the valley of dry bones.

It may seem a far cry from this type of sermon to the Devotional, but here, even more than elsewhere, we must remember what we have already said about sermons not being entirely monochrome. Indeed, all of them should be pervaded by the spirit of devotion. It is this that distinguishes them from merely secular discourses. The difference should be specially marked in the devotional or liturgical sermon properly so-called. Here the purpose is not so much to instruct the mind as to move the heart; it is the emotions, not the intellect, that are the particular point of attack. In this kind of sermon it is the preacher's especial aim to bring his people to love God rather than to know about him.

For this purpose the mental atmosphere is all-important. Prayers and hymns and readings will all help to create and maintain the right atmosphere, but the chief means will be the attitude of the preacher. I do not mean that he must put on any special voice or air of piety. If both were not completely natural they would defeat their own end. But I mean that he must be careful to preserve in his own person that attribute of awareness and response which is characteristic of genuine prayer. He must avoid any levities that he may ordinarily permit himself. He must try not to let any word or action or tone of voice strike a discordant note. He should as far as possible — I cannot too often repeat the advice — forget himself and be immersed in God. It should be evident that here all begins in God and flows back to God.

It follows that the structure of this type of sermon will be less formal, or at least less obvious, than it normally is. Suppose, for instance, that the occasion is Easter morning. What more appropriate than the note of thanksgiving? The preacher will be content to strike it in his opening sentence and to make every paragraph echo it throughout his address. He may illustrate it from Miriam's song of triumph after the victory at the Red Sea; he will capture its exultant joy as he stands in memory by the garden tomb on that first Easter morning; he will feel the up-lifting sense of power as he contemplates Christ's victory over death and hell, over evil in the world and in the hearts of men; and he will find it repeated as he joins on the other side of time "with all he loves and all he flows from soul in soul".

That is all that needs to be done in this kind of sermon. To sound the one note, to sound it loud and clear, maintains the unity of the service and makes it — what it should especially be on such an occasion — a paean of praise and thanksgiving. And that has the most practical of all results, in that it really does affect our attitude to the whole of life.

An occasion when the atmosphere of devotion is particularly necessary for both preacher and congregation is the Three

Hours Service on Good Friday. The fact that in recent years a number of more or less attractive services have been proposed as alternatives or substitutes for this 'Devotion' need not lead us to think that its usefulness is over.

Nor (to mention another reason for possible change) do I think we need be unduly worried by the suggestion that some of the 'seven words' can no longer be regarded as authentic. Actually, the question of the comparative historicity of these several sayings is very far from being settled. In the meantime, we can deal with them as part of the liturgy and use them with effect to stir up our own devotion. Certainly the liturgy in which we embody them is of the simplest — hymns and collects with intervals for silent prayer and meditation. Although it is not indigenous to this country, as is that other popular occasion the harvest thanksgiving (started by Hawker of Morwenstow in 1843), it has had a much longer trial, having been introduced by the Jesuits after the earthquake at Lima in 1687. In modern times it seems to have commended itself especially to Anglicans all over the world. Whatever may be the truth about the 'words', it is at least clear that they convey the picture that the second or third generation of Christians preserved of their dying Saviour. It is surely something gained if we succeed in seeing him through their eyes.

To preach seven or eight sermons on end is certainly a great strain on any preacher, but it need not be too great if he keeps the tone quiet, avoids excessive emotionalism, does not talk too much but preserves enough time between the addresses for the hymns, prayers and meditations (the last of which he may or may not conduct himself). The object throughout is to keep the mind fixed upon the crucified Redeemer and to appreciate the love he showed to mankind in his last prolonged agony. A very experienced preacher described his own aim in this service: "I just tell my people to gaze and gaze and gaze. That is really all I have to tell them."

In a Retreat or Quiet Day, much the same atmosphere of

devotion should be maintained, though here there will be a conscious effort to induce the hearers to examine their lives, ask what is God's will for them, and come to some determination about their plans in the immediate future. As an aid in this exercise the addresses may well contain some element of instruction, but it is the will, strengthened by the emotions, that is here the special point of interest.

Some conductors of such exercises are fond of basing their addresses on the exposition of one of the epistles or some article of doctrine. The difficulty is that in such a method what is primarily intended as a devotional address may easily become an expository sermon or a professorial lecture. For myself I should be inclined to recommend for such addresses a more general background in the whole Christian ethos. If one wishes to bring people to a decision, there is nothing quite so helpful as to make them ask what all their religion is about, and then to find within that general scheme an answer to their own particular question. In such an enquiry there should be plenty of scope for good resolutions. If that scheme holds good for the retreatants, I am sure that a bird's eye view of the whole Christian stance is bound to be good for the conductor.

As for basic guidance on the best method of conducting retreats, I know of nothing to equal the *Spiritual Exercises* of St. Ignatius. No doubt psychologists will continue to say that his scheme is too weighted. No doubt, too, the preacher is certain to find the outline too full and elaborate for modern taste. To the first objection I would reply that a retreat is not an exercise in philosophy or logic, and to the second that it ought to be quite easy to catch the spirit of St. Ignatius's method and to adapt it without attempting anything like slavish imitation of his scheme in detail. A knowledge of Ignatius ought to help us to preserve the atmosphere of devotion, while leading our retreatants to definite decisions.

To return to our main topic of subject choice. The preacher should always bear in mind the duty of finding a place from time to time for what is called a Mission sermon. By this term is meant a sermon whose specific intent is to convert the unbeliever or to transform the 'uncommitted' into the fully practising Christian. In days when the West was generally regarded as necessarily Christian it may have seemed natural to leave this precise function to 'foreign' missionaries or to preachers at street corners, but that is no longer possible. Almost everything in our environment conspires to remind us that the unbelieving world is crowding in upon us. The atmosphere in which we live is increasingly sceptical, or at least cynical, and the traditional moral standards, as is well known, are in danger of becoming submerged in a 'permissive' society.

This change in the temper of the times has had one good effect: it has sharply reminded the Church of its primary duty. That original and most significant task is not to look in upon itself and nourish a society of saints: it is to go out into the highways and hedges, the board rooms and common rooms, and to win a fresh fellowship for Christ. Only then can the Church begin to build its members into that communion of saints which is the Body of Christ. To find representatives of the 'uncommitted' it is not generally necessary to go beyond the church doors. The preacher will find some, though perhaps not so many as formerly, within his own congregation, especially among the more casual members of it. To them he must assuredly address himself from time to time, deliberately attempting to win them to a more wholehearted acceptance of the claims of Christ.

In so doing he will be following the example of the earliest church. The first Christian preachers seem to have won their converts mostly from the attenders at the local synagogue. It seems natural that we should have our most marked success among those who have not cut themselves off entirely from us. So, occasionally at least, the parish pulpit should extend an invitation to all who have not yet done so to commit themselves to Christ without reserve. The mouthpiece of this invitation will be fulfilling the original intention of all preaching: he will be proclaiming the good news; he will be issuing a challenge; he will be the voice, the triumphant voice, crying in the wilderness, "Prepare ye the way of the Lord."

One objection regularly levelled against mission preaching is that it is too emotional. That no doubt is why so many preachers label their special efforts in this direction as 'teaching missions', wishing to assure the staider element among both clergy and laity that there will be some appeal to the intellect as well as to the feelings. The caution is made necessary by horrific stories of the hysteria following upon such mission efforts as those of Wesley and Whitefield, as well as more modern experiences such as that of the Welsh Revival, which have led quite serious enquirers to ask the question, 'Pentecost or Bedlam?'

In the past, psychologists as a body have, on clinical grounds, voted heavily against this type of preaching. It is, however, only fair to add that in more recent days some psychiatrists have defended it on the ground that it is not unlike their own method of 'shock' therapy. In cases of severe aberration, they say, it may prove the only effective treatment. Perhaps an answer would be that they are medical men and can adapt their treatment to the individual, whereas the preacher is at best an empirical psychologist, dealing with people in the mass. Most of us would probably agree that no preacher should deliberately incite his hearers to the point where reason loses its control. The discovery that he possesses power to do so may be as bad for the preacher as its exercise may be bad for the congregation.

Does such constraint rob the preacher of his chief instrument for conversion? By no means. The fear of hell, the dread of temporal punishment, even the revolt against one's own past have ceased today (whatever may be true of former times) to be among the chief levers in the movement towards repentance. The main cause of individual conversions is the appealing figure of Jesus seen in the crib or on the cross, upon the mountain or in the homes of the sick and unfortunate, but always against the background of our common human life.

Even the attractiveness of Christ, which must always remain the mission preacher's strongest ground of appeal, is by no means the only one. Many are still attracted by the excellence of Christian moral teaching and see in it the only hope for mankind. The fact that fresh matter for debate is always cropping up in the ethical field does not obscure the recognition that with Christianity a new moral force appeared in history and that our best energies are still devoted to the effort to assimilate it. Even a permissive society sometimes feels a yearning for the deep-seated purity of Christ. The hippies' ideal is essentially an appeal to what they believe to be the character of Jesus as against the formalities of the so-called Establishment.

Another objection often alleged against mission preaching is that it fails to make its converts persevere. Because its appeal is so largely to the emotions, and because human emotions are as unstable as the sea, a mission's influence is likely to be evanescent. For this reason the wise preacher will pay considerable attention to the environment in which his people live. The school, the office, the home, the factory are not always within his immediate reach, but the many organisations (clubs, scouts, guides, Mothers' Union, G.F.S., Bible Class, etc.) run by the Church are. He should do his best to see that they take a sympathetic part in his work of conversion. They should provide a welcoming home-away-from-home for the new convert and help him to grow in the faith he has now embraced. After all, these institutions are an example of the friendliness, awareness, and eagerness of the Christian life, or they are nothing. They should be the visual aids to the parson's preaching, the nursing mothers of his spiritual children.

The need to enlist the environment in support of the preaching is less recognised in England than on the Continent. In this country we have been accustomed to make a somewhat sharp distinction between religion and other social forces such as culture and politics. Other countries may find it advisable, for instance, to run religion and politics together in order to ensure sufficient scope for the highest influences. And so they form Christian Democratic parties of one kind or another. We, however, while we congratulate ourselves on having representatives of religion in all the parties, actually resent (quite unreasonably), any 'interference' of religion with politics, no doubt confusing 'politics' with 'party politics'. Again, on the Continent the interaction of religion and culture is generally recognised even where it is resented, while we are scarcely willing to admit any vital connection between religion and painting, architecture, the theatre, ballet, and most of the arts.

The result of this dichotomy is that we seldom think of conversion except in terms of the personal relationship between the individual and Jesus Christ, whereas on the Continent (particularly in France) conversion may be the result of a changed attitude to the whole of life, or even to one element of art or culture. I am not suggesting that in the preaching of conversion one can bypass the person of Jesus, who is indeed the basis, soul and centre of the Christian life; but God has more than one way of leading men to himself, and his fishermen should spread their net as wide as possible. Quite apart from personal allegiances, one may come to believe that the hope of mankind lies in a religious rather than a secular interpretation of the universe, and decide to give oneself to its propagation. It is well known that such an evaluation of the environment was responsible for many conversions in nineteenth-century France and it is still the explanation of occasional Christian recruitment from among the intelligentsia. Such people really have come to believe in Christianity as the only hope for the world. In any case the preacher has to think, like St. Paul, not only of the Jesus of history but also of the universal Christ. It is a point of view that has hardly yet penetrated to the pew.

This reflection leads to a final word about mission sermons. They should generally include, and should sometimes be wholly devoted to, the discussion of apologetic questions. No one today can be unaware of the widespread doubt about the veracity of the Christian faith. That doubt may be the result of environmental pressure (many homes today are quite irreligious), or of unfortunate personal experience ("Why has God done this to me?"), or of intellectual doubt (compare the prevailing historical scepticism). The preacher may be morally certain that, for whatever reason, some proportion of his congregation will be in need of reassurance.

His main difficulty, which applies in a measure, as we have seen, to all preaching, will be that the people he addresses will think on widely different intellectual levels, and will show widely varying capacity for the assimilation of new ideas. It is this lack of homogeneity that makes necessary a very special caution on the part of the preacher. While some of his hearers will be impatient of what appears to them unduly old-fashioned, others will find the same material quite frightening in its novelty, and neither side will be slow to express its resentment. One way out of the difficulty is to remit the serious discussion of problems such as these to the Bible class or lecture room. Another is to present opposed views side by side without formal decision, merely pointing out that "some people say this and other people say that", and leaving it to those who are interested to ask questions at another time. Two things at least are abundantly clear: that we must never show our cleverness by cramming half-baked novelties down hearers' throats, and that on the other hand we must never again let our congregation fall several generations behind in its knowledge of the Bible and of current teaching. The parish priest's own growing experience will teach him not to strain his people too high for too long or, *per contra*, to earn their disdain by presuming to talk down to them and treat them as children.

One thing he must try to do for them all, and that is to wean them away from the idea that somewhere just around the corner awaits the perfect truth which, if they can only find it, will demonstrate the unmistakable certainty of their religion and set all possible doubt at rest. There is, actually, no such proof, and if there were, it would undermine the whole nature of Christian faith. We are set in an ambivalent world; a secular and a religious explanation can be found for anything under the sun. It is the preacher's duty to show that the religious explanation is actually more reasonable than the purely secular, and to induce his hearers to make the leap of faith necessary to grasp it and commit their lives to it. Always we must remember that faith is the Christian's métier; the just shall live (not by sight) but by faith.

We have been speaking so far as if the only type of conversion here in question was the change of mind that leads to all-round acceptance of the Christian faith. Actually there are other kinds of 'conversion'. In medieval christendom the *converti* were not the pagans who had been won over to Christianity, or even the apathetic Christians who had just awakened to the meaning and claims of the religion in which they were nominally involved. The term was applied to those in whom a new sense of vocation had been kindled, and who had passed from life in the world to life in a religious community: the 'religious' were the monks and nuns. It is the duty of the clergy to keep alive in the minds of their people the possibility of such a vocation for themselves. The preacher's is the voice of the Church. It is through him that we are authoritatively bidden to examine our own conscience in the sight of God to find out what is his will for us and for the purpose to which we shall devote our lives.

If this is the case with the invitation to the 'religious life' technically so called, what about vocations to the priesthood or the ministry in general? Where are the succeeding generations of pastors to come from, if not from among those who are privileged to hear the challenge from the pulpit and to obey it?

It would be a dereliction of duty if the clergy did not use the opportunity afforded by the pulpit to repeat the challenge and so help to fill up the vacancies in their own ranks. There can be few greater happinesses for a preacher than to have been instrumental in calling some of his own faithful into the sacred ministry.

And what is to be said of that ministry overseas which used to be called 'foreign missions'? In spite of the fact that the world has grown so much smaller; that there is no longer any 'darkest Africa' but only 'developing countries', that the Esquimaux are already Christian, that the erstwhile aborigines of Australia are nearly all gathered into missions and settlements; that what used to be called 'romance' has so nearly died out of the whole gigantic enterprise of Christian missions, there are still many places where the adventurous and independent spirit may find its own opportunities of doing God service. But how shall they preach except they be sent? And who shall send them unless the preacher first reveals to them the possibility of this vocation for themselves?

I began this letter by putting myself in the position of the man who is trying to make up his mind what kind of sermon he shall preach. I have mentioned a few possibilities, but by no means all. What I have tried to do in effect is to remember how wide is the field. Religion is in fact as large as life itself. There would be little cause for boredom in the congregation if the preacher would remember how extensive and varied is the commodity he has to sell. The agent of a large firm does not limit his sales talk to one small section of his firm's operations. On any computation we are the accredited agents of one of the greatest corporations the world has ever known. If we cannot be familiar, or deal adequately, with the whole range of its operations, we can at least help our people to realise that their feet are set in a large room. Whoever finds life too cramped, it should certainly not be the Christian or his teacher.

At the centre of our world stands the figure of the Christ.

He is himself the universal personality; it is he who opens the gates of new life to us. In introducing people to him we shall make clear how rich is the life and how varied the opportunities to which he calls them.

LETTER 11

Preparation of the Sermon

My dear Robert,

Having determined what kind of sermon, out of the several classes described above, he wishes to preach, the speaker must now come to grips with the preparation of the actual discourse. If the theme has already been dictated for him by some special circumstance such as a festival or a request from some deserving charity, the first step is quite easy. He will look at the lessons from scripture appointed for the service and find some passage that may fit the appointed theme. If, however, the theme is not already fixed, he will look still more carefully through the lessons to see what subject they suggest for explanation and comment. At this point he may well feel as he did in his student days, when he first looked at an examination paper and could find in it nothing whatever to suit his taste. In that case the only thing is to look again and to look more deeply. He will soon find that some message stands out both for himself and for his people.

When he has thus found his theme and the passage in which it is enshrined, he will need to narrow down the latter to a text. That text may be used either as a point of departure or as a succinct summary of the sermon. It may be selected because of its epigrammatic quality, or for its omnibus character, or simply because in striking words it presents a direct challenge to the hearers. Some preachers deliberately choose a short text the oddity of whose phraseology can be relied upon to attract attention, while others will take a complete paragraph and use

96

the whole of it as basis for the sermon. The range of choice in any case is almost infinite, particularly if one does not stick to the lections for the day; but it must not be thought for this reason to be a matter of indifference. The selection does give the tone for the rest of the discourse; it is the element most likely to remain in the memory; and if it is well chosen it may well prove to be a sermon in itself.

When he has chosen his passage, theme and text, the preacher may feel able to jot down one or two leading ideas at once. Whether he does so or not, before going further he should allow time for the subject to simmer in his mind. Time is really of the essence. That is why one should begin thinking about next Sunday's sermon on the Monday previous or at latest on the Tuesday. (Of course there are special occasions when one needs much longer.) It is surprising how fresh ideas accumulate with each succeeding day. Here the non-manuscript preacher has an advantage over his manuscript-reading colleague. The former can introduce fresh ideas or add new material almost to the moment when he mounts the pulpit steps, whereas the latter, having once got his speech on paper, feels a natural reluctance to make drastic changes. In either case some period of gestation will pay handsome dividends in speeding up the actual composition of the discourse.

The next step for both men, having allowed as much time as they can respectively afford for their ideas to fructify, is to make a careful outline of the sermon. This we have discussed before; all we need do now is to remind ourselves once again that the outline should be kept as clear and simple as possible. For the so-called extempore preacher, the outline will not be so final as for the reader. The former will no doubt alter his outline frequently, as later thought enables him to enrich it and improve upon it. One has heard of those who will make as many as twelve such outlines before hitting upon the one that seems least unsatisfactory. (I put the matter thus negatively, because I think that the man of conscience and taste will never be completely satisfied with his work. All he can hope to say in the end is, "Well, this is the best I can do.")

The writer, having once made his outline, must, as a general rule, stick to it, for now he takes his most important step: on the basis of this outline be begins to write his sermon. Some preachers like to take plenty of time over this task, working it in among the bits and pieces of multifarious parochial duties. Others like to deal with it in one fell swoop, setting aside for it one morning in the week which they keep free from all other tasks.

What of the non-manuscript man during this time? If he is experienced, he will probably be using odd moments of his time to go over his outline, improving it, filling it in, or committing it to memory. He thus becomes so familiar with it that he can see his whole composition, as an architect may see his building or an artist his pictures, in one vivid flash of imagination before it is a physical reality.

But what if he is not experienced? Here I want to make a suggestion, which may seem to contradict much of what has been said already, but which I believe nevertheless to be of first-rate importance. Every young preacher should write out his sermons *in full* for the first ten years or so of his ministry. I do not mean that he should read them from the pulpit or learn them by heart. Why then should he write them? Because that is the best specific against mere garrulity. The effort of writing is a good discipline for any speaker. As he writes, he can think over his words, change, choose and polish them as no extempore speaker can ever do, unless of course he is painfully slow. Similarly with ideas: no writer could bear to labour long at his task unless he was producing something in the way of thought, whereas the rashly extemporary speaker has often nothing to say and says it for far too long. That is why the natural speaker needs the long discipline of composition: its restraints will teach him to speak more nearly as he writes. This he must learn to do, if possible, without losing the direct, vivid and even vehement approach that distinguishes the orator as against the writer.

While he is revising his outline or writing his manuscript, the preacher will be continually asking himself how he can make his sermon interesting. In an ideal world, no doubt, it would not need to be *made* interesting. If one remembers the circumstances of the original proclamation of the good news, one can hardly believe that it could ever become less than interesting in its own right. Happily there are times in the experience of most people when that still proves itself true. But the world has heard the same message proclaimed daily for two thousand years, and most of us have listened to it as long as we can remember. The result is that the fine cutting edge of it has been dulled. The preacher must therefore exercise all his ingenuity to present the message clear, sharp, and alive.

It is quite fundamentally important that the sermon should be interesting, for without such incentive the attention is bound to flag and the effort will be wasted. Fortunately there are some writers who seem to have the gift of being naturally interesting. "One good thing about me," a young writer was heard to say, "is that I simply cannot write a dull line." He was lucky, but there are some orators who seem to exercise the same natural attraction over their audiences. It must be a happy feeling for such a man when he notices the instant quickening of interest on the part of his hearers the moment he opens his mouth and begins to speak. All he has to do now is not to let slip the attention he has been spontaneously accorded. And that is sometimes the more difficult part.

What it is that gives to some men this astonishing facility of address it is not easy to say. One might hazard a guess that they are on fire with the message they have to deliver, and that by some freak of telepathic communication their enthusiasm kindles a spark in the audience even before they begin to speak. Let us admit at once that very few of us are like that. The born orator is as rare as any other kind of genius. Let us also recognise for our comfort that the most effective speakers, the ones who have really changed the course of events, are often not born but made. From Demosthenes to Winston Churchill, they have often suffered from some physical defect which they had, through patient effort, to overcome. Happily most of us, even if we have not been granted the original gift of genius, have at least been spared the handicap of a hampering defect. We can always reflect that the bulk of the world's soundest work is done by second-class men. Perhaps the reason is that they have to work harder to get their results. We had better settle down, then, to cultivate such gifts as we have, and to look around for any help we can find to make our sermons attractive. Here, again, you will find your teaching experience quite invaluable.

We have seen that our task is to make the old (and perhaps tarnished) truth shine with a new, uncommon lustre. If the bare statement of fact has, through constant repetition, lost the sharp edge of its appeal, we must provide it with a point that will touch people 'where they live' and stab them broad awake. This we can sometimes do with the judicious use of illustrations, similes, quotations and anecdotes. I am well aware that such a method can be grossly overworked, and that few sermons can be so wearisome as one that is nothing but a string of stories. But before we condemn the method out of hand we should remind ourselves of the example of Jesus and his parables. Nor do I think that we need pay much attention to the objection that this method is scarcely honourable in that we are actually 'eking out our copper with other men's gold' and often, at that, without acknowledgment. A sermon is not a theological essay written for other specialists, in which we are expected to state all our sources in order that the experts may verify them. We are working for the salvation of men's souls and all is grist that comes to our mill, so long at least as we do not infringe the law of copyright.

At the same time we must never allow the accumulation of

anecdotes to obscure the essential attractiveness of the message itself. Stories and illustrations should not be too numerous, and they should be thoroughly germane to the subject in hand. The preacher must not give the impression that he has become so disillusioned about the power of his proper message to attract that he has let himself fall into the position of a public entertainer. Whatever may be the truth about the preaching friars of the Middle Ages and the popular preachers of Victorian times, the world of entertainment today is crowded with professionals who are likely to be much better at their own job than we are. It is much better for us to stick to the task for which we were ordained and to remember that the gospel must always be presented as a challenge as well as good news.

One fact that may well encourage circumspection in the use of anecdotes and stories is that they are not readily repeatable. I have already suggested in an earlier letter that the congregation, especially the unlettered portion of it, is much more likely to remember your stories than your general ideas. The former will be easily recalled (and perhaps even resented, if they appear a second or third time), while the latter may have to be repeated many times before they sink in. The lesson for the preacher is not that he should eschew altogether the use of illustrative material, but that he should use it sparingly. Like jokes, anecdotes may be very effective when used singly, but used in the mass they tend to neutralise each other and their effect is spoilt. This warning applies especially to anecdotes about oneself. If the preacher may legitimately draw upon his own experience to prove a point, he should still keep personal reminiscences to a minimum. Any minister who draws undue attention to himself is betraying the Master who sent him. Everything, *everything*, in the sermon must point to Christ, and any adventitious aids are meant simply to help the hearers to fix their attention on him.

Some preachers, desiring to keep their hearers' attention while avoiding such simple methods, cultivate a highly paradoxical method of speaking, exaggerating grotesquely or just turning common statements inside out. The method used to be employed with great effect in the literary field by such writers as G. K. Chesterton, Oscar Wilde, and G. B. Shaw. But it is generally inappropriate in the pulpit. Its danger is not only that, like all exaggerations, it may quickly pall, but also that it violates literal truth, and so may undermine the credibility of the speaker. And if that is lost his influence has gone with it.

To return now to our apprentice preacher, whom we left tackling the task of writing out his sermon in full. All I have done in the last few paragraphs is to offer him some advice as to possible ways of presenting his message faithfully without losing its essential challenge. No one would be so foolish as to suggest that success in this endeavour can be easily won, but after all he is dealing with the most important thing in the world; so it is worth while to take some trouble over it. Naturally in writing he will follow the outline he has already prepared, but he will not scruple to depart from it if he thinks that further thought has now enabled him to improve upon it.

When he has finished the script, he will probably lay it aside with a sigh; but not, one hopes, for long. Even if he is going to read it in the pulpit word for word, he should make himself thoroughly familiar with it, so that he can not merely read it smoothly but actually preach it with force, accuracy, and lack of hesitation. It is just as well also for him to make sure that his manuscript is intact. It is said that Winston Churchill, speaking at a City dinner, found himself reading a passage twice over. He realised that his secretary had omitted to remove the carbon copy, and turned the contretemps to his advantage by observing, "You will not have failed, gentlemen, to notice that I have repeated my last few sentences. I can give you no stronger assurance of the importance I attach to the point I am trying to make." However, his situation was less trying than that of one of the Australian State Governors, who, reading the Queen's speech at the opening of the local parliament, inadvertently turned over two pages at once. His mistake led to an interesting legal argument whether the business mentioned on the missing page could legally be transacted during the ensuing session.

The lesson is that if we are to use mechanical means at all we must see that they are in good running order. This applies not only to manuscripts but also to such things as microphone, desk or cushion, platform (if any) within the pulpit, and everything else that may make the difference between good and bad reading. Some of these things are not under the preacher's immediate control, but his manuscript is, and he should take care that it is as perfect in every way as he can make it.

But what of the non-reader? He too, in the early stages of his career at least, has been busy with a manuscript: can he afford to let it lie idle in the drawer, there to remain imprisoned over the ensuing Sunday? By no means. When he has finished writing it, he must make a fresh outline from it, making sure that he has got the logical sequence right. I do not recommend that he try to learn the whole script by heart, though some very fine preachers have done just that. Some phrases, particularly at the beginning and end of the discourse, may well be treated in that way, but generally it is safe to rely on the inspiration of the moment and on his vague recollection of the script for the actual words, so long as the thoughts have been assimilated in their proper order. For this purpose he must have the outline firmly printed on his mind. Whether he takes the half-sheet of notepaper on which he has recorded it into the pulpit with him or not does not really matter. One day he may become so experienced that he need never in the preparation of his sermons set pen to paper at all. He will still need to have the outline fixed clearly on the retina of his mind so that he can follow it point by point as he preaches. He will then be heartily thankful that he has learnt to keep his analysis simple: it will make things so much easier both for himself and his congregation.

Still thinking of the non-reader, there is one other element in the *mise en scéne* to which I ought to draw attention, and that is the lighting arrangements. Generations of churchwardens and sidesmen have become so accustomed to the needs of the manuscript-users that as soon as the sermon begins they have all the lights turned down except that in the pulpit, which they actually reinforce. I tremble to think how many devoted servants of the Church I have upset by reversing these arrangements. For one thing, a bright light in the pulpit hurt my eyes and for another I needed to see the faces of my congregation. This is surely one of the instances in which we do not have to follow the custom of the theatre. Actors do not wish to see their audience, but they do want their audience to see them. The preacher, on the contrary, has no particular desire to be seen, so to speak, in detail by his hearers, but he does want to read the expression on their faces and so to judge what is their reaction to his words. How can any orator adapt himself to the situation, if he cannot see the faces of the people to whom he is speaking? At any rate, every visiting preacher should be carefully asked what he wants done about the lights while he occupies the pulpit.

Having considered the traditional methods of sermon preparation, one may well ask whether modern facility in invention has not produced something that will ease the preacher's burden. There is at least one appliance that has been found useful by a few, especially among the extempore preachers, and that is the tape-machine. Bishop Joost de Blank, whose preaching brought back vitality to the church of the East End after the devastation and exhaustion of the Second World War, regularly used such a machine. Having fully prepared his sermon by the method described above, he would preach it to the machine and then play it back to himself as often as he needed it for further correction and assimilation. It certainly proved beneficial in his case, but I am bound to say that, having given it a brief trial, I abandoned it as useless to me. Perhaps the lesson is that each preacher should shop around and find the precise method that suits him best, and then stick to it until it becomes part of himself.

In any case, he must never begrudge the amount of time spent in the choice of his subject and in the actual preparation of his sermon. Nor must he ever be afraid of adopting a thoroughly professional attitude to his task. After all, this is God's business and it demands the very best that any man, however talented, can give to it. His own painstaking care will never preclude God's gift of a special charisma of inspiration.

LETTER 12

Delivery

My dear Robert,

Since we have sat so long with the preacher in his study preparing his sermon, it seems logical that we should now accompany him to the pulpit and see how he 'delivers' it. One does so with some reluctance, and that for two reasons. First I share to the full the Englishman's classic unwillingness to discuss (except in the music-hall) another man's physical traits and habits, and, second, I recognise that there is absolutely no specific for making any particular person attractive or even acceptable to others. Perhaps the most one can do is to learn how not to draw attention to one's own peculiarities. "Pause, pause, my brethren," said a young preacher as he spread his enormous hands over the pulpit shelf, and then wondered why the young people laughed out loud.

It is certainly not in order to make the preacher self-conscious that one ventures to discuss this aspect of his work, but on the contrary to help him lose any obvious trace of self-consciousness. He can hardly hope not to feel nervous; and indeed, if he has a proper sense of the seriousness of his task, that feeling will remain with him to some extent all his life. But to appear too much at one's ease might be a thousand times worse. One can appreciate the complete aplomb with which young artistes appear on the silver screen, without wishing to see it reproduced by the deacon in the pulpit.

So let him be his natural self, relaxed and unafraid, resting secure in the knowledge that God is with him. "Underneath are the everlasting arms." Let him stand quietly without fidgeting, his body straight, his feet firmly planted on the floor of the pulpit or its platform. Pop singers may introduce variety in their performance by wandering all over the stage, but the parson must learn to live at ease within the narrow confines of the modern pulpit. An actor, if he does not know what to do with his hands, may light a cigarette or pour himself another drink, but the preacher may always find a rest for them, one on either side of the pulpit desk. If he is a reader, the question hardly arises, because his hands will be largely occupied in turning and smoothing the leaves of his manuscript. If he is not a reader, his hands will be free to perform such gestures as come naturally to him. But they should be natural and not forced. Public speakers are not naturally natural: they only become so by learning to think more of their audience than of themselves.

Perhaps the most natural of all gestures is the admonitory forefinger. But not too much of it, please. It is very putting off if a congregation finds itself being treated like a class of naughty children. The stock of authority was never so low as it is today, and it is more important than ever for the clergy to show themselves, without becoming servile, the servants of the servants of God. In any case, there are plenty of other gestures that suggest themselves. A very experienced preacher used to recommend that, if a speaker found the attention of his audience inclined to wander, he should, with an inviting circular motion, place a forefinger on his lips. The idea was that the motion would draw attention to the source from which his words came and so to the words themselves. It sounded to me ingenious, but the only time I ever tried it I felt so foolish that I never repeated the experiment.

Gestures are most likely to be natural if they are used sparingly. They should, in other words, be replicas of the gestures we most commonly use in ordinary conversation. Since no two people are precisely alike in the way they move their hands, the gestures come to have an additional advantage in so far as they reveal the character of the speaker. They should therefore count for at least something in helping the congregation to understand what kind of person is speaking to them. And, if he is honestly trying to live up to the gospel he preaches, he need not be afraid of such a disclosure. When all else fails and a particularly nervous preacher has still not learnt what to do with his hands, he can always put them behind his back. That is a quite good stance in itself until it gets tiring, and then the hands will appear of themselves and quite unconsciously take their part in the general delivery of the sermon.

The hands are not the only members of the body to render important service to the preacher. Equally deserving of consideration are the eyes. This has not always been recognised. In the old days the custodians of some large church would tell us solicitously that we should be heard all right if we kept our eyes on such and such a point on the west wall, or on such and such a tomb in the north aisle. Their advice was probably valuable in the days before the microphone came in, because each building has its own peculiar acoustic properties. But the advice had one great drawback: it tempted the preacher to keep his eyes glued on one particular spot, and that an inanimate object; whereas his gaze ought surely to be roaming at large over his audience. No doubt a great deal of nonsense has been written about the power of the human eye; nevertheless, it remains true that it is a very powerful instrument in the control of attention. What sort of rapport can there be between preacher and congregation if they cannot look each other in the face?

Naturally, as we have already noticed, this use of the eyes is not easy for one who is reading a manuscript. But it can be done. Some preachers become quite clever at appearing, while still reading, to be giving their undivided attention to their hearers. The secret of this magic I have never discovered, but I should think it has a good deal to do with being thoroughly familiar with one's script before stepping into the pulpit. In any case, it is a faculty that readers should carefully cultivate. No speaker is likely to be very effective with a large audience if he is obliged to keep his head down and his eyes glued to the paper before him. Certainly any preacher who has groups of children in his congregation will do well to keep his head up and his eyes open.

This brings us to the most important instrument of all, namely, the voice. It might be thought that the need for special care at this point had been made unnecessary by the introduction of hearing aids and amplifiers, but that would be a great mistake. It is true that the advent of the microphone has made us less anxious about the carrying power of the unaided voice. It is no longer necessary to advise the speaker to 'address the deaf man on the back row'. That was not very good advice anyhow. If you got the volume right for the deaf man on the back row it was likely to be very uncomfortable for people on the front row. And what right had the deaf man to seat himself so far from the speaker? He might at least have had a little sympathy for the preacher's pharynx.

The appearance of the loud-speaker and the microphone has not made care in the use of the voice unnecessary. In fact, it has actually demanded more care, if not in control of volume, at least in clarity of enunciation. Most people have to cultivate a little extra precision when speaking down the telephone; so must the preacher who has a microphone in front of him. Especially this is true of final syllables and consonants. Slovenliness in this respect is unfortunately part of our national heritage. The Frenchman who noted that Englishmen, wanting to buy a well-known dessert fruit, generally asked for 'a basket of strawbs' was a shrewd observer. Unless we take special pains, the microphone is likely to exaggerate this fault. How many words, by the way, does one miss on television?

The benefit which the microphone has really conferred is to take care of the long-distance part of the business. In the old days the inevitable tendency on the part of a man confronting a considerable audience was to lift up his voice and shout. Today, if he does that, he will choke the instrument and the whole performance will become absurd. Nowadays, what he needs to do is simply to speak a little more slowly, a little more clearly, and a little more loudly than he would in ordinary conversation. The machine (if it is functioning properly) will take care of the rest.

But that is not quite all. It is not only the machine that must function adequately, but also the human instrument. The preacher must know how to manage his voice. No doubt in these enlightened days he will have received some instruction on this subject in his theological college. He may even have been sent to a professional voice-producer. I am always a little nervous about them. Their interest seems to be centred mostly on the stage, and it is for the stage that their technique is specially devised. They have very little knowledge of the peculiar acoustic properties of Gothic buildings and still less of the numinous quality of the liturgy. I am very far from belittling the elocution of our great actors. One has only to listen to them declaiming a speech of Shakespeare or of G. B. Shaw to realise what a glorious means of communication the English language can be. In this respect I put them *hors concours*. But after all they are actors; they are trained to act a part. And that is a thing the parson must never do. I am always interested to notice how, when actors are asked to read a lesson in church, the best of them leave behind all the special arts of the theatre and fall back upon the quite fundamental rules of good voice-production, without any attempt to be specially impressive.

It is this fundamental technique that the preacher must learn. As a matter of fact, I should be inclined to advise you to ignore the professional and to be content to trust to good taste and common sense, if I did not know them to be quite insufficient guides. A good deal of what the preacher needs does not come by nature, but by art. It is not natural to stand haranguing a whole crowd of people, and if one is going to do it as a lifetime business one must learn above all things how to produce one's voice. For this purpose I recommend you to have some good singing-lessons. As you are an Anglican you will have to do a good deal of intoning anyhow, and so in learning to sing you will be killing two birds with one stone (if that is not too unkind a way of putting it). Three things at least you will learn in singing: to listen to your own voice; to breathe properly; and to distinguish between the head- and the chest-register. All three are of first-class importance for a speaker.

We are accustomed to ridicule the person who is too fond of the sound of his own voice. His complacence may be due to the fact that he has never been taught to listen to it critically. It is important that he should so learn, because only he can tell by what precise infinitesimal movement of muscles in mouth and throat changes in the quality of his own voice are produced. It is actually more a feeling than a hearing, and that is why mere listening to a tape-recording of one's voice, though valuable, is not enough. Indeed, most people when they first hear their voice played back to them do not recognise it as their own. One simply must get used to listening to oneself and *feeling* the vibrations as one speaks.

Then we have to learn to manage our breathing. We all have a tendency to revert to a childish habit of breathlessness, especially when we are nervous. The remedy is to draw the breath deep down, thinking of the lungs as pear-shaped with the broader end at the bottom, and it is more sensible to get a good store of air into the capacious part between the ribs than to exert undue pressure on the narrower part at the top. Sixty and more years ago our teachers used to enforce this lesson with a horrific story of an Italian tenor who tried to produce his top note by the wrong method and dislocated a collar bone. If we can get the feel of intercostal breathing (and even the athletes have to use it nowadays) we shall soon learn to keep the air down and prevent it from rushing to the throat. If we do continue to close our throat in order to hold the breath there, we shall probably produce a parson's voice, laryngitis, and various other unpleasantnesses for ourselves, with consequent effects upon our congregation.

The third thing we learn is to fetch the voice from the place where we have stored the air rather than from the top of the skull, where presumably there is no such storage-place at all. This means that we must speak from the chest-register rather than from the head-register. You can tell the difference by contrasting the voices of children at play with that of your favourite bass singing 'Down among the dead men'. It is extraordinary how often this simple difference is ignored. One has known preachers who have gained a quite undeserved reputation for being querulous or 'sissy', when all they have been doing is to produce their voice wrongly. And *per contra* one has known quite prominent people in public positions who have learnt the lesson late in life and have had the courage to change their method with excellent effect.

Resisting the natural temptation to pitch his voice too high, and refusing to strike a note, the preacher avoids giving the impression that he is about to declaim. He thus fits into the pattern of preaching as it is practised today. We are much more conversational than our predecessors used to be. Undoubtedly there were great orators in the past, and their speeches still remain as monuments of literature; but their sentences would sound like so much bombast if addressed to a modern audience. In any case, if you are going to speak in the grand manner, your words must be in the grand manner too, and few speakers nowadays would be prepared to risk the dangers of Augustan prose. We may go so far as to say that oratory in the classical meaning of the word is dead. Winston Churchill was the last who consciously followed that ideal, and even he was capable on rare occasions of breaking down in a period and coming to a lame conclusion.

The modern preacher avoids periods and purple patches. He aims at being conversational without being chatty, although 'fireside chats' on the radio and television have set him the example to follow. So, to recapitulate, he talks in the pulpit as he would in a drawing-room, but slightly more clearly, deliberately and loudly. He is, after all, in command of the situation; if he has no applause to assist him he has no opposition to worry him. So he remembers at the outset to fetch his voice from somewhere in the region of his diaphragm and then forgets all about it. In other words, he is as natural as he can be, without appearing too much at home.

From this vantage point the preacher is able to avoid many of the problems that beset other public speakers. Modulations of pitch, pace and pose will occur simply as they are suggested by his words, and will not be studied or meretricious. The story of the old-time Evangelical preacher, whose manuscript was found to contain the stage direction "Weep here", must surely be mythical; but it is true that some speakers' emotional outbursts do give the impression of having been carefully studied; and that, of course, destroys the effect and undermines the would-be orator's influence. This seems obvious enough, but we must not go on from there to condemn all emotionalism in the pulpit. It is part of the preacher's fundamental task to move his people to sorrow for their sins, love for their neighbours, and adoration for God. It is difficult to see how he can do this without feeling these emotions himself. Indeed he must always pray to be allowed to experience precisely these feelings. "An audience will identify itself only with an excited man."* But, however hard it may be to define, there is a real line of demarcation between a false and a legitimate excitation. If the preacher is detected 'working himself into a state', it will certainly undermine belief in his sincerity.

Perhaps to this general description a word may be added as to the particular question of speed in utterance, which in itself is generally taken as some indication of excitement. We are always being exhorted to speak slowly. This may be good advice, because our tendency, particularly when nervous, is to speak

* Peter Brown, *Augustine of Hippo*, p. 252.

with more than usual rapidity. But the slowing-down can be carried to intolerable lengths. A legal luminary of the last generation, who had also a great reputation as a political speaker, was asked how one should regulate one's pace in speaking. His reply was significant. "You should speak each sentence slowly enough for your audience to anticipate what is coming, and then you must conclude it better than they have already done it in their own mind." It is just possible that that kind of thing may pay dividends in Parliament or on the platform, but it would never be tolerated in the pulpit. Benches are hard and children are restless; there are very few congregations that would put up with a really slow speaker.

At the same time, one whose own temptation has always been to talk much too fast has good reason to point out how easy it is to fall into the opposite error and, by excessively rapid speech, to prevent the audience from gathering much of what you wish to teach. All of us have suffered from missing half a comedian's jokes because we cannot keep pace with him. He at least has the excuse that he must keep things moving or the excitement he is trying to build up will be lost. We, on the other hand, are trying to help people to absorb eternal truth, and that takes time. We should therefore allow sufficient time for our words to be grasped and their meaning to be divined, without becoming either portentous or boring.

You may think that all this worry about practical details is going to be fairly embarrassing when you get into the pulpit. I agree, and for that reason I repeat my advice to get as much practice in public speaking as you can before you are ordained and commit yourself finally to your career as a preacher.

LETTER 13

Today's Need

My dear Robert,

Preaching, to be effective, must be contemporary. It must appeal to the condition of the current generation. A bishop, occupying the pulpit of a university church in the Michaelmas term, and taking the opportunity to castigate some undergraduate vices, was said to have arrived a term too late: the people of whom his allegations were true had disappeared during the long vacation, and a quite new generation with different characteristics had taken their place. In the great world outside the colleges, changes do not occur quite so rapidly as that; but there are changes, and no one generation can be profitably addressed in terms that would have just suited another.

Any preacher may make his sermon appear contemporary by the illustrations he uses and the idiom he employs. But this in itself is merely specious. If he wishes to appeal to a congregation 'where they live', he must understand the way they think here and now. He must know what are the actual difficulties they experience and what seems to them most 'real'. In other words, he must address himself to today's needs.

The needs are always changing, but the peculiar difficulty for the parson is that, quite apart from any dictation by his own tastes and character, he is addressing several generations at the same time; he ministers to all ages from the tiny tots to their great-grandparents. William Temple, preaching to the school at Repton, could say that he always talked to the fifth and sixth forms and left the rest of the school to pick up what crumbs they could. A school is a very closed society and it was no doubt possible to make up elsewhere to the younger members what they missed in chapel. But the parish priest stands between the old and new, between the Victorians and the *avant garde*, and in order to keep the family of God together he must interpret the one to the other and gently lead both along the upward path. Somehow he has to explain the one to the other, and the gospel to both. He must persuade them to seek a common salvation.

This is more easily said than done; the differences today are so acute that those who display them appear to belong to separate worlds. Even the use of the word 'salvation' will come with something of a shock to those who are already accustomed to think in the new terms. Nor will the differences be made less acute by the fact that the number of the *avant garde* in the congregation may be quite small in comparison with that of their more slow-moving brethren. Indeed, the separation may become more marked, if the parson himself has wholeheartedly embraced new methods of study, and finds himself at a loss when speaking to people whose whole stand on religion is rooted in tradition.

Such separation is the cause, not only of mutual distrust and suspicion but also, in general, of our modern malaise. Ever since we realised that we must learn to read the Bible 'like any other book', the scholars have applied to it the sciences of historical and literary criticism. In the elements of these sciences, as thus applied to their own foundation documents, most of the clergy have been trained; but they have not, as a rule, thought it necessary to teach them to their people. The relevance of such subjects to practical religion seemed so remote as to be excusably ignored. The result has been to widen the gulf between pew and pulpit, so that if the preacher does have occasion to refer to such matters, he finds himself talking in a language not only strange but even terrifying to a considerable proportion of his audience.

The long-term solution for this state of things is to catch the hearers young, and train them early in the new methods. Some steps in this direction have been taken in schools and colleges, but the difficulty there is to find enough teachers who are themselves sufficiently versed in the new methods adequately to educate their pupils. Before the generation gap could be filled we have been overtaken by a new advance in scholarship, which has dissipated what used to be called 'the assured results of criticism', and has gone far to undermine the historical basis on which the evidence for Christianity presumably stood. This movement of thought is not confined to theological interests alone but has affected the reliability of all historical research. It is the prevalence of historical scepticism (or agnosticism) that forms the biggest obstacle for the Christian apologist at the present time.

It seems odd that this should have happened just at the time when the reading public has been provided with the greatest variety of excellent translations of the scriptures into contemporary English that has ever been published. It had been thought by many that, if only the archaic speech of the Authorised Version could be made to give way to the colloquialisms of everyday speech, everyone would at last understand his Bible and all would be well. But things have not turned out quite like that. It has been discovered that it is not only the idiom but also the thought of the Bible that is difficult. In spite of the fact that several of the new versions proved to be 'best sellers', the effort required to understand the Bible has once again proved too much even for some of its well-wishers.

This is a gloomy and partial view of the situation: it is by no means the whole truth. In addition to the schools, colleges and universities, there are many voluntary organisations, such as the extra-mural lecture courses, the Christian Education Society, the William Temple colleges, whose work has been directed precisely towards filling the gap in theological knowledge between the generations. Their efforts have resulted in the gradual development of a more receptive attitude both to the

Bible and to Christian doctrine, restraining the too drastic revolutionism of adventurous spirits and reviving the courage of those too fearful of undermining the faith of the weak. Already there is a steady increase in the body of those whose moderate opinion recognises the paramount importance of religion in private and public life, and is ready to use modern methods of study in vindicating it to themselves and others.

One of the signs of this type of thought is its refusal to join in the search for some logically invulnerable proof of the certainty of the Christian creed. The prevailing mood of historical agnosticism has at last made us face this question, not merely in the lecture-rooms but also in the churches. We have learnt to recognise that, if faith is the Christian's métier, he cannot expect to live by mathematical certainty. It is obvious that, when certainty comes in, faith goes out. If certainty is possible, there is no room or excuse for faith. As far as religion is concerned we are back in the position of Tennyson's Ancient Sage,

> For nothing worthy proving can be proven
> Nor yet disproven.

But if we cannot *prove* the 'truths' of the Christian creed, we can still defend their credibility: we can show, or at least try to show, that they are reasonable. They do not, when they are studied in their proper context, offer an affront to our intelligence. While acknowledging that there are at least two ways of looking at everything, we can still conscientiously contend that our way is the better. We leave it to the Holy Spirit to turn this contention into conviction.

We can adopt such a method with the better conscience because it is the Bible's way. The writers in both Old and New Testaments recount great historic events and give their own explanation of them. If the Israelites were saved at the Red Sea while their enemies were drowned, it was because God controlled the waters. If Jesus appeared again after his death, it was because God had raised him from the tomb. Similarly God's guiding hand was seen not only in outstanding historical events, but also in the ordinary occurrences of everyday life. So we are encouraged, whenever we have to choose between alternative explanations of temporal events, to accept the one which, while not excluding 'natural' causes, still allows of God's controlling interest in human affairs.

Nor need we be unduly distressed if some faint element of doubt still lingers in the mind. Faith takes its leap, not, as is often said, in the dark, but in the half-light of reason. It is an effort, not of the intellect only, but of the whole man, including will and affection. It is not just a movement of the logical mind accepting a proposition, but of trust and love for a living person. That kind of allegiance, once given, is continuously renewed and maintained as the result of personal experience. It implies that we interpret all natural phenomena and all natural events in the light of what we believe to be God's good governance of his universe. That is the kind of faith we have to nourish, throughout our ministry, in ourselves and in our people, and to show as clearly as we can that it works out.

No doubt a foremost place for discussion of this kind of topic can be reserved for the bible class, study group, or any other organisation that springs up in the parish to further an intellectual approach to religious problems. It is there that one meets the section of the community that is most anxious to learn and is therefore least likely to be disturbed by any new alleged fact that is presented to it. True, the teacher is hardly likely to anticipate the scare headlines in the papers—the speed of modern journalism in gathering news is too great for that—but if he has got some way in the training of an intellectually minded nucleus, they will have been forearmed against the latest news that the Bible is not true, or that Jesus never lived, or that God is dead.

In any case the preacher cannot confine his attention to the out-and-out believers among his flock: he must spare some thought for the hesitant and the doubters. He should bear them especially in mind now and then, as I have already suggested, in one of his routine sermons. To feel that he is dealing with matters of life-and-death importance to some at least of his hearers will give life and vigour to what the preacher has to say. He may be surprised later to find out as a by-product how much interest he has stirred up among the more faithful members of his congregation. Even the traditionalists sometimes appreciate a spring-cleaning among their ideas. They like to see the old truths shining with fresh brightness in a revised context.

It should even be possible from time to time to deal immediately with some issue that has aroused the notice of the Press. But here a word of caution is necessary, especially if the issue is, or appears to be, a new one. In such a case the first reaction is generally violent, and may be made doubly so by the exaggerated or ill-informed way in which the first report has been presented. Not many journalists are expert theologians, and they can hardly be expected to detect the subtle distinctions with which the specialists will almost certainly have hedged about their original report. In dealing with such a matter from the pulpit, one must take more than usual care to speak with sympathy and understanding. A denunciatory attitude is not as a rule strikingly helpful.

In this connection it is also worth remembering how quick is the Press to fasten on any suggestion of disagreement between leaders of opinion: the fiercer the argument the more fodder for the newspaper men. One cannot altogether blame them for this. Reporters have to send in a story, and they have to do their best to make it lively. Human nature being what it is, public attention is much more easily attracted by news of a storm than by a report of peace along the whole front. The latter is so nearly equivalent to 'Nothing to report'. So, if it has been found impossible to preserve intellectual harmony among ourselves, the preacher ought to do all he can to avoid exaggeration or over-emphasis. The pulpit is not usually the best place in which to air family grievances.

But to return to our main theme. Normally, any instruction of an 'apologetic' character will be given in one of the lecture-sermons already described, or even in a whole series of them. This does not mean that the subject should be excluded from other sermons. On the contrary, a great deal can be done in occasional paragraphs to strengthen intellectual grasp of the faith and to enlighten knowledge of the true character of Christian doctrine.

Considerable help can be given by way of illustrations drawn from Church history. A cordial may be provided for some drooping spirits if it is realised that there never was a time when all followers of Christ thought and said the same thing. Scholars have long recognised, for instance, that each of the writers of the New Testament had his own individual point of view. The golden age of the peace of the Church is not in the past, but in the future. We must learn to be of the same mind even if we are not of the same opinion.

Not that we want this kind of teaching to turn into some rather second-class theological lecturing. We have to remember that we are not lecturing but preaching. Some members of the works-staff at a great cathedral criticised a learned and historically minded preacher. "We don't want to hear about all those old chaps; we want something that will do us good today." Such timely warning should help us always to keep before us 'Christ and him crucified'. Every word we say is intended to point to the Saviour and to challenge our hearers to put their trust in him.

It may help us in our apologetic efforts if we remember, even in our present condition of doubt, that the ultimate victory is on God's side. We must not give the impression that we are fighting a losing battle. The best means of defence is attack. By the very variety of our preaching, uniting so many themes in the one figure of Christ, we show that the universe belongs to God.

What, in any case, is the alternative? Who would want to live in the kind of world without God depicted in so many of our modern plays and novels? In spite of all their brilliance and permissiveness, the world they show us is far less 'liveable in' than an ordinary Christian home where love is. That is the kind of home that the majority of the public still wants and needs.

The New Testament represents Jesus as carrying on a running fight against the demons, the spiritual hosts of wickedness, all through his ministry. His potential victory was made clear in the words with which he replied to Satan during the special temptation in the wilderness, and its crisis was successfully passed in the cry of triumph from the cross, *Consummatum est.* The mopping-up operations have continued ever since in the ministrations of the Church and will not be ended until this world has ceased to be. In those operations (whatever may be the significance of the demonic) our preaching forms a conspicuous and necessary part. We must take care that it is carried through in a proper spirit of confidence. "If the trumpet gives an uncertain sound, who will prepare himself for the battle?"

Confidence is a spirit that is conspicuously lacking in our day, especially among the younger clergy and those who are in training to join their ranks. I still have a painful recollection of the young priest who was being interviewed on television and, when asked how he would describe the *differentia* of his profession, could only reply, "Well, I have more time." One wonders how the television authorities manage to find such inadequate representatives of the clerical profession. But indeed there are only too many who have so failed to solve their own difficulties that they have no clear guidance to give to others. We have to recover the consciousness of being engaged in an age-long campaign. The demons against whom we fight today are not only those of moral delinquency but also those of ungodliness, the out-and-out atheists, and even more the agnostics who undermine the faith of others by shrinking from taking sides. No doubt some at least of them are thoroughly conscientious and have thought things out as well as they can, but find themselves able to come to no definite conclusion. We can acclaim their sincerity and commend them to the love of the God in whom they cannot believe, but in the present context they must be seen as on the wrong side of the fence. As Montgomery said of his great opponent Rommel, after praising his skill as a soldier and his character as a man, "But of course he is still the enemy." However honestly we may admire some of the representatives of non-faith, we must never forget whose side we are on, or let sentiment excuse slackness and lack of moral courage on our part.

We shall find it a great help if we refrain from wasting time in denunciation, and adopt as positive an attitude as possible. To declaim about the emptiness of atheism or agnosticism is one thing: but it merely emphasises an aching void unless we still more vehemently proclaim the glories, present and to come, of the kingdom of God. However much each age is affected by its especial needs, the essential aim of preaching is always the same: to make men realise the fullness, the joy, the power, the usefulness of a life lived in allegiance to God. This is the glory of preaching, that it opens the gate of new life to those who accept the proffered key.

That is why there are still those who feel the same constraint as St. Paul: "Woe is me if I preach not the gospel." It is a divine impulsion: the bearer of good news cannot keep it to himself. The woman who said of her vicar, "That man would preach you into heaven if he only could," had a right perception. That is what we all, as preachers, would like to do, "if we only could", but, since the decision must be made by the man in the pew himself, and not by anyone on his behalf, we are compelled to adopt a humbler but still satisfying role—to point the way and help the wayfarer.

Let no preacher fall into despondency because he does not see results. It is true that he does not receive the immediate applause that buoys up the professional entertainer, but he has something much better in the prospect of lives changed and strength renewed. It may be rarely that specific examples of this effect are brought to his notice. But let him think in general terms of the harassed mother who looks forward to the Sunday sermon as an oasis in the arid desert of the week; of the businessman who sees his problems in a new light as he is led to view them *sub specie eternitatis*; of the school-leaver who, starting out on a new office job, finds her anxieties relieved as she is reminded of the everlasting arms; of the boy facing his O-levels and learning to view the prospect of success or failure within the overruling providence of God. It is not merely the impact of the finally polished sermon but the *obiter dictum*, the spontaneous but God-inspired phrase, that may strike a note or flash a light in the inner consciousness, and may remain as an impulse long after all the rotund phrases have been forgotten.

Nor must we disregard the influence of the preacher himself. In the long run it is less what he says than what he is that is important. The reason why we still have to emphasise the aspect of preaching as an art is that the real personality of the preacher must be allowed to shine through what he says. He must learn to express his thoughts in such a way that his utterances will not distort the true image of himself. Needless to say, this is not the man as he is by nature but as he has been remade by grace, the natural man redeemed and made the instrument of God's own purpose of communicating himself to others. If it is still true that religion is caught and not taught, it is all the more important that the preacher's personality, expressed in his words and gestures, should be that of a fully dedicated, God-inspired man. We *are* our preaching. That is why William Temple could claim that the sermon is itself a kind of sacrament, a sacrament of personality. On the other hand, if our sermons are careless and slipshod, the impression we are likely to give of ourselves and of the God we serve will be both uninviting and disheartening.

A recent period of theological thinking has taught the clergy to recognise that their fundamental confidence does not arise from any belief in their own capacity or ability, but from the fact that they have been called, chosen, and ordained by God himself. That was a salutary lesson, which has fortified many a man who, without it, might have found his burden too heavy for him to bear. Having made this impressive claim, we must now in the new age justify it by the seriousness we bring to our duties. In a world of professionalism we cannot afford to be excused as amateurs. Nor must we allow ourselves to be put off by what some unco' guid people say about the dangers of professionalism among the clergy. As Mr. Heath said to the interviewer who accused him of being a 'professional politician', "I am a professional and proud of it." If a well-known athlete can appear on a television screen and say proudly to a million viewers, "Football is my life", can we dare to say anything less of our own calling?

Preaching, it is true, is not the whole of that calling. There are other responsibilities of the priestly life that make demands on our time and devotion. But preaching is still the means by which we can reach the greatest number of people, and perhaps also the means by which the majority are still kept in touch with Christ. From the early days of Christianity the application of the term Word has hovered between the uttered thought of God and the human voice of his preachers. It is still the peculiar glory of our profession by the grace of God to keep the two applications of the term in mutual coincidence.

P.S.—On reading through this last letter I cannot help feeling that you may be disappointed because I have not ended on a more personal note. I hasten to make what amends I can.

I have honestly set out, as I see them, the conditions that a young man like yourself is bound to encounter when he enters upon his life as an ordained preacher. They are not all such as to cause doubt and despondency. It is true that if the thirteenth century could be called the age of faith, the twentieth must be called the age of doubt. But neither description is complete and both need a good deal of qualification.

In our own day we find that doubt is often only another name for a spirit of enquiry. What attitude could be more inspiring for one who desires to help others in the search for truth? My only proviso is that, if he is to be of real help to others, he must believe himself, in some sense at least, to have found the secret of the good life.

I do not deny that to say to an audience, "This morning I am going to invite you to join with me in a voyage of exploration" can be a most exhilarating introduction to a lecture or series of lectures. But it loses a very large part of its value if the audience does not guess that the lecturer knows very well already where he is going. I am very far from suggesting that before you undertake this ministry you should feel that you have a ready-made answer to every doubt and every difficulty, but I am quite sure that you should feel that you already have an answer to the riddle of the universe as a whole.

Nor do I feel that your answer should belong to that kind of demonstrable certainty with which we assert that two and two make four. But I feel that it should belong to that other kind of certainty with which you can pledge your belief in the integrity of some friend of long standing: "I would stake my life on his honesty."

Unless you have that kind of belief, I do not see how you can dare to offer yourself as a guide to the blind. The clouds from which the angels of the nativity spoke were not clouds of doubt nor mists of unbelief: they were clouds of glory and the glory was reflected in their message. It was a true, if poetic, insight that induced the poet Donne to compare with these angels in the clouds the preacher in his pulpit. He too has a positive message to deliver, a message of peace and reconciliation through the revelation given in God's Son. That is the message that the Church has conscientiously tried to convey to mankind through twenty centuries of varying struggle and success.

Appointment to ministerial office implies, among much else, that you become an accredited representative of this corporation, the Church. Having regard to what the Church stands for, this implies—and there is no escaping the implication—that there is a very real sense in which you claim to speak in God's name. It stands to sense that you must believe whole-heartedly in the existence of him in whose name you claim to speak. For the Christian this 'existence' includes a specific nature and personal being. On analysis, this concept may appear like a splintered diamond, each section displaying separate idiosyncracies and demanding separate examination. I do not say that you should be concerned about all these differences, or even that you should be capable of understanding them. But I do think you must have a basic conviction about the existence and character of God and about the bona fides of the society that professes to proclaim him.

Whether you have that basic conviction or not, no one can say but yourself. The claim to have it, which you publicly and formally make on your entrance into the ministry, means that you have made your decision and burnt your boats. Henceforth you cannot go back on it without surrendering the ministry that you have undertaken on that understanding. You are committed, and you cannot afterwards speak or act as if you were uncommitted. This is a serious matter, as serious as any with which you are ever likely to deal, but there is no need to be nervous or neurotic about it. You will have plenty of time to make up your mind during your years of training; and you are sensible enough to rely upon the steady set of your mind rather than on any fleeting wave of emotion.

Yes, it is a serious matter, but the rewards are tremendous. To have the privilege of helping other people—not casually, though that is fine, but as the main business of your professional life; to have young people coming to you for advice in their time of trial; to be looked upon by all and sundry, from the children to the grandparents, as their reliable friend and confidant; to bring comfort to others in sickness and bereavement; to bring inspiration to the young and courage to the elderly: all this is reward beyond price for a life-time's devotion. It implies, of course, that preacher and pastor are the same. And so they should be. But that is another story.